MODERN
BARBECUE
COOKING

By ED BELL
America's Foremost Barbecue Chef

Incorporating The Author's Famous
BARBECUE COLLEGE COURSE, Plus More
Than 200 Favorite Barbecue Recipes

Edited & Designed By
DON FITZGERALD

PACIFICA HOUSE, INC., Publishers

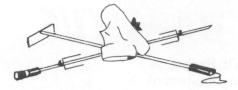

ACKNOWLEDGEMENTS
The author, editor and publisher of Modern Barbecue Cooking wish to express their appreciation to the following organizations for their contribution towards the production of this book, in text, recipes and color photos: National Livestock and Meat Board, Chicago, Ill., American Lamb Council, Denver, Colo., Poultry and Egg National Board, Chicago, Ill., Big Boy Mfg., Inc., Burbank, Calif., Kaiser Aluminum & Chemical Corp., Oakland, Calif.

EDITORIAL CREDITS
Cover color photography, plus center spread and other subjects in color section, Larry Harmon, Altadena, Calif. Pacifica House staff contributors, photography for Ed Bell's Barbecue College Course, Elton Sewell. Art illustration, Bob Johnson and Bernice FitzGerald. Copy staff, Liz FitzGerald, Patricia Arthur and Brigitte Wegmann.

MODERN BARBECUE COOKING By Ed Bell   (Title No. 103)
Copyright © 1966 by Pacifica House, Inc., Publishers
Produced and Printed in the United States of America

PACIFICA HOUSE, INC., Publishers

Publishing Offices:	Pacific Regional Office:	European Regional Office:
10000 Riverside Drive	1132 Auahi Street	85 Schuetzenmatt Street
North Hollywood, Calif., U.S.A.	Honolulu, Hawaii, U.S.A.	Basel, Switzerland

Contents

Introduction

When distinguished foreign visitors are entertained in modern America, the one festive occasion which surely will be on the agenda is a full-fledged barbecue feast. The ritual must, by tradition, be complete with the rich aromatic air of charcoal cooking, the succulent flavored meats, distinctive sauces and informal atmosphere of western outdoor cookery.

The picture is unforgettable to the guest of honor, indeed, typically American and fit for a king. But what the visitor probably does not realize is that this same festive setting can be, and often is, duplicated every weekend in thousands of American family patios. Yes, barbecue cooking is that special — yet that easy and popular! A truely masculine outdoor undertaking, barbecuing today has been elevated from a favorite hobby to a fine culinary art. Equipment has been perfected to perform at a "gourmet" level and recipes are readily available to match.

One of the most important influences on the popularity of barbecuing is the education of the public to the correct procedures of barbecuing. Foremost in this field is Chef Ed Bell, Dean of the BARBECUE COLLEGE and author of this unique book. Millions of Americans have been influenced by his "in person" demonstrations and tens of thousands have graduated from his instructional classes. Now, for the first time, Chef Bell has put his BARBECUE COLLEGE COURSE into text, coupled with more than 200 fine barbecue recipes. Drawing from the many questions most asked of him in the field, Chef Bell has condensed the instruction into the pure basics of barbecue cookery, as it is practiced with modern portable equipment, and using modern fuels and "everyday" supermarket foods. The result is the most complete and useful barbecue book ever published, and the first actually written by a noted barbecue instructor.

Whether an advanced student of barbecue cooking or a beginner, you will find many useful tips and suggestions in his course. The book will serve as a permanent reference volume as well as a recipe guide, regardless of your tastes, experience or equipment capability. It's theme is tastefully simple — learn to do it right, and every barbecue experience will be a rewarding success!

The Editor

Ed Bell's Barbecue College

Greetings:
We are pleased to have you among the prospective graduates of the BARBECUE COLLEGE. The next few pages, preceding the recipes, outline the basic procedures and theory of Modern Barbecue Cooking. It's really very easy to learn correctly, and we suggest that you stop reading now, unless you have at least 30 minutes to an hour to study the BARBECUE COLLEGE course uninterrupted!

If you are an experienced barbecue cook, you will find the study section an easy "refresher course." The beginner will be able to build a lifetime of rewarding barbecue experiences on the knowledge which he will gain from this short study course. Each chapter is presented as a unit, covering a single aspect of equipment, preparation, cooking theory, and "over-the-coals" procedure. Many cross-references are made between recipes and the educational text to better illustrate the point in question. Both the educational section and the recipe section have been designed to support and complement the other — assuring you complete understanding of every barbecue step up to the point where you "take off on your own" — the sign or complete mastery of the barbecue art!

History Of Barbecue

Barbecue cooking is man's oldest form of meal preparation. Prehistoric man was the first to barbecue. His cave fire served both to warm him and to tenderize the carcasses of animals caught in the hunt. With the advance of civilization to Greek and Roman times, barbecuing took on a new appearance. Adjustable grills and spit-roasting devices were found in the ruins of Pompeii. Castles of the Middle Ages featured walk-in fireplaces, large enough to roast whole animals over a wide bed of coals, as well as breads and other fare. French 17th-Century writings tell of the fine points of charcoal broiling fine cuts of meat (presumed steak) and joints of lamb and venison, "well basted in sweet butter." Here, too, was born barbecue sauce — for this same record calls for mixing wine vinegar, pepper, honey and orange juice with the meat drippings as a basting liquid and table sauce, vintage 1668.

Early Americans cooked over open coals and by adapting Indian methods and foods, developed the traditional Thanksgiving Day roast turkey — always barbecued until modern stoves came into being. Certainly the "West" was won over an open campfire and the culinary talents of those rugged outdoorsmen made a great contribution to America's appreciation of barbecue. Another important contribution to charcoal cooking in America came from the early Spanish settlers of the Pacific coast. Their rich seasonings and festive presentation founded what today is considered "western barbecue cooking." This same blend of Spanish flavors prevails today throughout the southwest, where barbecue is a favored ritual.

The name "barbecue" can be traced to several historical sources. One, easily credited to the western world, is from the island of Haiti, in the Caribbean, where it is native-talk for a ground-cooking rack, used over a simple pile of coals. The other goes back to 17th-Century France again, where the word "bebareacue" literally meant "cooking from beard to tail" to the Corsairs.

BARBECUING TODAY

A modern barbecue unit is now a permanent fixture in most American homes and patios. The barbecue art has come a long way from the cave man who had to cook over charcoal just to stay alive. Now it is the favored choice of families who want a change from ordinary "kitchen" meals — a festive flavor change which has become a modern masculine hobby. In fact, it's the only cooking chore that the "man of the house" can really call his own. Women, generally, just don't take to the equipment preparation, sooty charcoal, smoke and fire routine. But they surely enjoy the results as well as any man! Just look at the popularity of the fellow "who really knows how to barbecue" among his neighbors and friends.

Finally, barbecuing in the family patio or in the great outdoors, today is America's truly great contribution to the culinary arts. So typically American, it is a unique combination of our great natural bounty of fine foods, with the individual drive and imagination of each barbecue enthusiast. The result, Modern Barbecue Cooking, can take its place among the world's great cuisines.

Barbecue Equipment

Modern portable barbecue equipment comes in four basic classifications, picnic or table-top, braziers, barrel or covered units, and wagons. Of these, the smaller and easily carried table-top units are most popular, accounting for 44% of U. S. sales. Next in popularity are the larger brazier units, making up 32% of the market. Covered and barrel units account for 20% and wagons for 4% in sales popularity. Available from a number of manufacturers, barbecue units come in a vast range of sizes, shapes and prices. It is most important that the buyer of a new barbecue unit understand a few basic facts about quality, versatility and price before making any investment.

SELECTION: A quality barbecue unit, either large or small, will last for several years if properly handled and stored. While many inexpensive models appear elaborate, chances are they will not last through a single season. Here are a number of details about construction, size, accessories and capabilities which should help in selecting the proper unit for your barbecuing needs and to match your skills.

TYPES

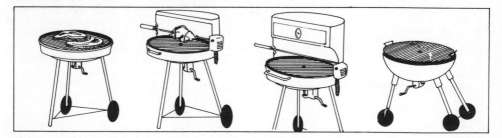

PICNIC & TABLE-TOPS: These are the most portable of all barbecue units, ranging in size from 12 to 18 inches in diameter in round braziers, comparable dimensions in rectangular units. Most are light weight with steel fire bowls. Some have collapsible legs. Better models have adjustable grills, wind screens and kebob skewers. Hibachi units also are included. Prices range from $3.00 to $7.00. Ideal for patio, beach, vacation and camping — also hors d'oeuvre cooking.

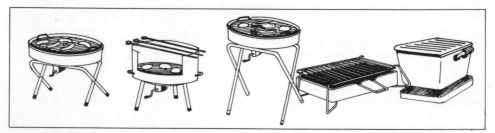

LARGE BRAZIERS: These include the popular 3 & 4-leg round bowl units, with or without hood. All better models have adjustable grills, wheels on two legs and rotisserie spit and motor. Some have warming ovens in the hood top. Some brazier units have collapsible legs. Ideal for family patio cooking of all grilled or open spit recipes, serving up to 12 persons. Prices range from $10 to $35.

BARRELS & COVERED UNITS: Starting the deluxe or "gourmet" line, barrel and covered units come in several shapes. The most popular is the barrel, set on four legs with wheels, and with rotisserie spit and motor. Others are rectangular or spherical with doors, lids or covers which close completely. They are designed to hold the heat and fumes in and around the food for faster cooking and better flavor. Far less fuel is required than on open brazier units. Deluxe models have built-in electric fire starters in the hood which also can serve as a cooking element. With the hood or cover open, these models are efficient grill cooking units. The grills are generally stationary, with the fire box, below, adjustable for heat control. Excellent for all large roasts, poultry and fish, as well as casseroles and vegetables. Roasts may be cooked on grill or spit when covered. Also good for smoke cookery. Generally a patio unit, those with electric element may be used indoors with very little charcoal (see Covered Cooking chapter). Prices range from $25 to $100.

WAGONS: Usually heavy and elaborate, wagons are not as popular as in past years, the barrel and covered units being more portable and less costly. Most units have large adjustable grill areas, extra storage cabinets, work boards, and warming ovens. Some have lids which will close for covered cooking. Limited to patio use, they generally require large wheels for easy moving, can cook for a crowd. Prices range from $60 to $250.

BARBECUE

Buying Tips

WHAT TO LOOK FOR: Here are some quality construction features which should be remembered. Sturdy steel fire bowl construction should be required. Finish should be baked enamel — some units are porcelainized, though they may chip or splinter if damaged. Grills, spits and spit forks should be heavy-chrome plated. Grill adjustment mechanism should be sturdy and preferably of the crank type. Motors should be heavy duty, "UL Approved" and capable of turning 15 to 20 lbs. of meat. Some inexpensive motors will turn only 8 to 10 lbs., then burn out. Spits should be sturdy enough to hold an 18 lb. turkey or ham without bending. Hood should cover at least 50% of brazier bowl on round units to hold in heat. Legs should have strong, secure fastenings to prevent wobbling or possible collapse of unit while cooking. Barrel and covered units should have tight-closing cover with plenty of room inside for meat to turn on spit. Adequate air vents should be at upper and lower portions of covered units. Fire box should be of heavy steel so that it will not warp with intense heat. Most heavier units should have at least 2 wheels for easy moving — the larger barrel and wagon units, 4 wheels. Beware of inexpensive imported units.

CARE AND CLEANING BARBECUE EQUIPMENT

A little extra care, along with knowing the proper way to use your barbecue unit, should keep it working well and looking like new for many seasons.

LUBRICATION: Like any fine piece of equipment, with moving parts, it should be lubricated periodically. Wheel axels need a few drops of oil inside and out, as does the spit motor (use label specifications). A little heavy grease on the lift crank mechanism or grill adjusting parts will keep it moving free and easy.

WIPE CLEAN: A properly prepared fire bowl, with foil and gravel liner (see Preparing Fire Bowl & Pan), never should burn out or have the paint scorched or burnt away. It also will stay cleaner as grease and smoke is kept at a minimum. After cooking is done, and fire extinguished (or briquets removed), simply wipe metal surfaces with a damp cloth. If greasy, use warm water and a little detergent. Finish with clean water and a wipe with a dry cloth.

GRILLS & SPIT: Grills should be removed from the heat as soon as cooking is complete. A quick wipe with a wet cloth while they are still warm, will probably remove most particles. If grills were properly wiped with oil before cooking, they will always clean easily. If crusted use warm water and a bristle brush. Steel wool or a wire brush should be used only as a last resort, to protect the chrome finish. Spits and spit forks should wipe clean with just detergent and water. Never use abrasives on painted or plated surfaces. Built up grease and grit may also be removed with most oven-cleaner preparations then rinsed clean and dried. The best way is always to do it as soon as possible after use.

STORAGE: After unit has been cleaned and wiped dry, cover with a light canvas cover if stored outdoors. Always remove motor and store it indoors. If possible, store unit in garage or dry shed. Collapsible units may be hung on a wall hook. Some barbecue enthusiasts like to build a small shed especially for their unit, fuel and accessories. The drier the storage, the longer the unit will last and operate efficiently.

RECOMMENDED BARBECUE ACCESSORIES

The following accessories and specialized equipment will make your barbecuing experiences more efficient. They are actually necessities for the expert barbecue chef.
BARBECUE TONGS — for turning foods and handling fuel.
ELECTRIC STARTER — for starting fuel correctly.
FIRE RAKE — for positioning fuel and tapping off ashes.
SPIT BASKET — for rotisserie cooking of small and delicate foods.
HAND GRILL — for easy handling of small steaks, sausages etc.
INSULATED MIT — for handling hot equipment and foods.
PLIERS — for tightening spit forks, handling spits.
MEAT THERMOMETER — for determining correct doneness in cooking.
BASTING BRUSH — (non-plastic bristles) for sauce basting.
BUTCHER CORD — (heavy string) for tying rotisserie foods.
EXTRA SPIT FORKS — for securing additional foods on spit.
HEAVY DUTY FOIL — (see Aluminum Foil In Barbecuing chapter).
CLEAN CHICKEN WIRE — for support in barbecuing seafood.

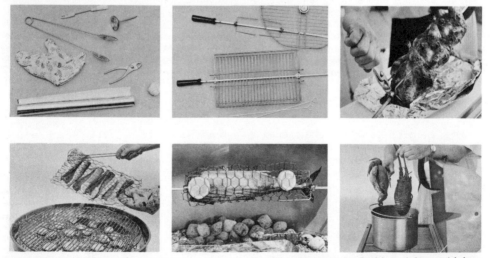

In addition to commercial barbecue accessories, other aids may be fashioned from chicken wire for fish cookery. Also, a large kettle on the grill makes a lobster and crab steamer.

Foil In Barbecuing

Barbecuing today without aluminum foil is as old-fashioned as making your own charcoal from sticks. Not since the introduction of the portable barbecue itself, has a single product so revolutionized charcoal cooking. Modern aluminum foil is present or has taken a part, in virtually every barbecue meal — from preparation and cooking, to serving and storing. This clean, fireproof, pliable, tasteless and inexpensive kitchen wrap has become more than just an aid or accessory. A roll or two stored with your barbecue unit is a must! Here are some facts and tips about foil and barbecuing.

SIZE & WEIGHT: Always select heavy-duty (broiling weight) foil for barbecuing. The standard kitchen weight is too light and will not stand up to heat, handling and shaping as well as the heavy-duty foil. Always select the 18″ large roll to avoid unnecessary patching and sure-seal wrapping. Generally, a double thickness of foil is adequate for most barbecue purposes, such as bowl lining, grill pans, food wrapping, grill covers, preparing foods to be cooked in the coals, etc. A single sheet is adequate for many "warm-up" recipes such as seasoned breads, buns, fruits etc., which are heated on the grill. Drip pan construction, however, requires four layers of foil for strength (see Foil Drip Pan). Whenever items which may have sharp bones are wrapped in foil, such as chicken or fish parts, always wrap a small extra "pad" of foil around the sharp spot to prevent it from puncturing the outer wrapper during cooking and handling. Remember to always turn foil packages with tongs or mitt during cooking — never with a fork or sharp instrument.

SHINY & DULL SIDES: All aluminum foil today is manufactured with a shiny surface on one side, dull on the other. This is important to remember as each surface has a particular duty to perform in barbecuing and should be used correctly. Like a mirror, the shiny side reflects heat and infra-red rays. It should be placed shiny side toward the heat whenever reflection is desirable — in lining the fire pan, in fashioning loose covers for grilled foods, wind screens etc. Many spit cooking units will be more effecient with a section of foil fitted around inside the hood, shiny side facing the spit, to reflect additional heat.

The dull side of foil absorbs heat and should be placed on the outside, or towards the heat, when something within the foil is to be heated. This is why all foods for foil-cooking among the coals or on the grill should be wrapped dull side out. This would include recipes for breads, baked potatoes, corn and all vegetables, fruits, some meat combinations and "warm-up" dishes.

WRAPPING FOR STORAGE: Clean, strong aluminum for foil makes an excellent wrapping for most foods to be frozen or refrigerated, including barbecue leftovers. By fashioning an "envelope" with folded edges, instead of just pressing edges together, a complete seal can be attained to hold flavors and moisture in, unwanted odors and air where they belong. Most foods may be wrapped directly against the foil. Some foods, however, which contain acids, such as tomato sauces, citrus juices or vinegar, may tend to deteriorate the foil and cause discoloration or harmless "flaking" to appear after a day or so. To prevent this, pre-wrap foods in waxed paper or place in a kitchen bowl before sealing with foil.

Fire Bowl & Pan

Like the foundation of a house, the base preparation of your barbecue unit prior to fire building is among the most important steps in charcoal cooking. Upon the simple task of lining and insulating the fire bowl or pan, rests the difference between the clean and rewarding results of the expert chef and the smoke and fire ordeal of the unknowing beginner. Here too is the secret of keeping equipment clean and free of excess smoke and grease, and like new for years longer. A properly prepared fire bowl will never scorch or burn out. Food cooks properly over the correct heat and far less charcoal is required. Here too is the end of "flareups" and smoke-crusted steaks!

FOIL LINING: The first step in preparing the fire bowl for brazier units (regardless of size), or the fire pan on barrel and wagon units, is to fit it with a foil lining. Use heavy-duty aluminum foil only, and in the long (18") size roll. Pull out enough foil to make a double-thickness liner which will cover the entire bowl. It is important that the shiny side of the foil be up to reflect heat. Large bowls may require an additional double-thickness of foil to reach all areas. Press the foil securely around the lift-pin guide in the center of round braziers, leaving the whole covered. The liner should fit tightly to the bottom and up the sides almost to the rim, folding all odd corners under to make a neat edge.

GRAVEL BASE: On top of the foil liner, pour in enough clean, dry pea gravel (¼" in diameter), vermiculite or prepared barbecue base material, to cover the bowl. Gravel should be about 1½-inches thick at the center of a brazier, feathering to 1-inch deep at the edges. Barrel and wagon fire pans require about 1-inch of gravel overall. Be sure that the foil is pressed against sides and gravel is smoothed all the way to the edge. Punch a hole through foil for grill lift pin. Your base is now ready for firebuilding.

HOW IT WORKS: The gravel base acts to hold the briquets away from the bowl, both for insulation and to allow air to pass under and up through the briquets, which are placed evenly over the gravel once ignited. This "breathing" effect assures even burning of fuel and spreads the heat out uniformly throughout the fire bowl or pan. With briquets spread an inch or more apart over the gravel (see Fire Building Chapter), 85% of the meat juices drip onto the gravel, not the burning briquets. This eliminates "flareups" and keeps smoking at a minimum. The flat surface of the gravel also allows the cook to position briquets easily with tongs, and it collects ashes. The foil liner below, automatically reflects what heat is projected downward, returning it to the cooking area for faster cooking and less fuel waste.

PERIODIC CLEANING: A properly prepared base should not be changed after each cooking. Leave it in the bowl. In fact, it may serve well for months, depending on how much grease is absorbed. Once the gravel becomes grease-filled, it may be poured into a bucket and cleaned with hot water and detergent. Rinse well and dry thoroughly before replacing on new foil. Damp gravel should never be returned to the barbecue, as it may explode when heated. Vermiculite or other porous base materials should be discarded, along with the foil, when grease-filled.

CAUTION: As mentioned above, wet or damp gravel may explode if it comes in contact with hot briquets.

Charcoal & Briquets

CHARCOAL & BRIQUETES

The main reason modern Americans cook over charcoal is for flavor! And the most important factor in good-flavored barbecuing is the fuel. All of the sauces, marinades and seasonings in the pantry can't compete with the aromatic richness of cooking over fine hardwood charcoal briquets, with maybe a few hickory chips tossed in for good measure. For this reason, as well as safety and economy, it is very important that the proper fuel be selected. With a good understanding of fuels, every barbecue experience will be a success.

SELECTION: Packaged charcoal and briquets come in a wide variety of qualities, prices, sizes and shapes. And since this book deals exclusively with cooking on modern portable barbecue equipment, we recommend that only premium quality hardwood briquets be used! Natural chunk charcoal, if made of real hardwood, can give excellent results, but inconsistent size and texture can result in uneven temperatures — and there is the constant danger of sparking and popping. Premium quality charcoal briquets are made of fine hardwood, pressed together with a starch binder. Uniform consistency assures even burning over a maximum period of time and with a minimum of smoke. Inferior fuels, briquets with little or no hardwood, are generally unreliable and in some cases, actually undesirable. While more expensive per bag, quality hardwood briquets actually are more economical in the long run, since fewer are generally required for the same amount of cooking. Read the label — see that it is made of hardwood!

CAUTION: Many cut-priced briquets, and even some expensive brands, are made from soft woods (which impart undesirable resins and tars) and even impregnated sawdust and anthracite coal. Others are made from fruit pits, sugar cane, corn stalks and paper products. It is important to remember that the pure hardwood charcoal flavor, that we so prize in barbecue cooking, can only be imparted into our foods through use of genuine hardwood briquets! Inferior briquets, bound together with petroleum products, actually can impart an oily film and unpleasant flavor to foods. Soft or inconsistent briquet texture results in uneven burning, excessive ash, and smoking. Inferior briquets also absorb moisture and may be difficult to light or keep burning — even break or explode during cooking. The selection of improper or inferior briquets is the greatest cause of barbecue frustration and failure — the cook is beaten even before he gets to the recipe.

STORAGE AND RE-USE: Always store briquets in a dry place. Even unopened bags can absorb moisture. Use a large can or pail with a tight lid, or seal opened packages in large plastic bags.

CHARCOAL IS FOR OUTDOOR COOKING ONLY!

Caution — As charcoal and barbecue briquets burn, carbon monoxide gas is released into the air. Highly dangerous if inhaled in a closed room, always remember to have adequate ventilation if barbecuing in closed quarters. If you must cook indoors, place unit in fireplace hearth or near an opened window or door. It is recommended that charcoal cooking always be done outdoors, where it is perfectly safe.

A possible exception to the rule is with covered or barrel units. which are equipped with electric charcoal starter elements. These elements may also be left on during cooking for the majority of the cooking heat, and just a few briquets used for flavor. This barbecue procedure may be undertaken indoors, but with adequate ventilation.

Fire Building & Starters

As soon as a barbecue cook has mastered the technique of starting and maintaining his charcoal fire, he is well on the way to completely successful outdoor cooking. As mentioned in Charcoal & Briquets the fuel is more than just the cooking medium. It is directly responsible for the flavor and texture of the food. But most important, the charcoal alone, and how it's handled, controls the temperature and cooking time, something to remember from the very start of your fire building!

THE CORRECT AMOUNT OF FUEL: Most inexperienced barbecue cooks use far too much fuel. In fact, they litterly "burn their foods to a crisp" over coals hot enough to stoke a steam engine, then wonder why it's charred on the outside, raw inside. This error is easily corrected by figuring the exact amount of fuel required for the job. For brazier grilling, unlighted briquets should be positioned over the firebed with an inch or more space inbetween. This will adequately cook a full grill of steaks, chicken, ribs, etc., with a burning time of up to 1½ hours. For spit cooking, a double row of coals should be positioned together along the back edge of the firebowl under the hood. Large roasts or poultry will require a second or third layer for longer burning — up to 2½ hours. Barrels and covered cookers require far less fuel, and will be detailed in Covered Cooking.

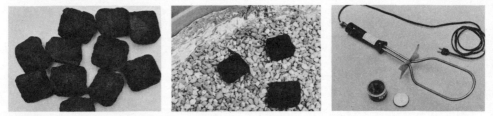

STARTERS AND BRIQUET STARTING: This course recommends only two modern methods of fire starting as completely safe and taste free. They are the electric starter and the use of jellied alcohol (chaffing dish fuel). While many charcoal starter products are popularly sold, none are reliably safe for family use and free of aftertaste. Commercial starter fluids, so widely used, are generally petroleum products and can be dangerous if not used absolutely according to instructions. Oily film and undesirable flavors can result also, if the fluid is not completely burned away in the lighting process. Never use raw gasoline, alcohol or kerosene, all of which will explode — and never add more starter fluid of any kind to briquets which have been started and appear not to be burning. They probably are burning and a serious accident could result!

ELECTRIC FIRE STARTING: Start your fire about 30 minutes before cooking. In an open section of the fire bowl, pile briquets into a pyramid directly on the gravel base. The electric starter element should be placed just on top of the bottom layer and covered on top with the remaining briquets. Plug in starter and allow 5 to 10 minutes for spots of gray ash to appear over about ⅓rd of the surface of the briquets. They are now burning properly. Remove starter element and repile briquets using tongs. They should be completely covered with ash about 20 to 30 minutes after starting. Briquets are now ready to be placed in position for cooking.

JELLIED ALCOHOL STARTING: Start your fire about 30 minutes before cooking. Pile briquets in a pyramid pile, directly on the gravel base, and spoon two or three ½-tea-spoons of canned jellied alcohol (chaffing dish fuel) into openings at the lower edges of the pile or part way up the sides. Remove and close fuel can before igniting jelly with a match. When a gray ash covers most of the briquets, after 20 or 30 minutes, arrange in position for cooking. Note: No additional jellied fuel should be required and remember — briquets are burning when even the smallest spot of ash appears.

LIGHTING PROBLEMS: Charcoal briquets may be difficult to light if damp or wet. Lighter fluids will not help start them either, if wet — so always keep briquets in a dry spot, ready for easy lighting. Wind also may retard starting. Attempt to screen off the wind during the first few minutes, though once the gray ash appears, a little wind will act to speed up the burning.

REPLENISHING FUEL: Recipes which require long periods of cooking over medium or low heat, may require that fresh fuel be added midway through cooking. If only a few additional coals are required, place unlighted briquets at the edges of burning fuel, then move to cooking position when ignited.

FLAMEUP CONTROL: Flameup may occur, even with a properly prepared fire base if coals are placed too close together, or if meat being cooked has an excess of dripping fat. This is easily controlled with a household water sprinkling bottle.

EXTINGUISHING COALS: When cooking is complete, burning briquets may be extinguished by several methods. As mentioned in the Charcoal & Briquets, they may be placed in a metal container with a tight lid — the lack of oxygen will extinguish them quickly. On barrel or covered units, simply close all dampers and vents — the coals soon will go out. Never spray or dump water into your barbecue unit. The steam and heat will damage the moving parts and corrode the finish of most metal units — as well as create a grease-soaked mess!

FUEL QUANTITY & POSITION

MORE OR LESS FUEL: The basic rule of barbecue temperature control is the simplest! Add more fuel for hotter cooking — remove fuel if too hot. Also, the closer briquets are together, the hotter the cooking. Use tongs and experiment with your particular unit. You soon will be able to control it to within a few degrees of perfect cooking temperatures.

DISTANCE FROM COALS: The easiest way to make fine adjustments in cooking tempera-ture, once the proper bed of coals is burning, is to change the distance from the cooking food to the fuel. Most brazier units have adjustable grills which will allow up to six inches or more of control. Barrel and closed units generally have fixed-height grills with adjustable fire pans which offer the same control. Most of the recipes note distance from coals in instructions. Other temperature terms noted are, "hot coals" (grill 3 to 4 inches from coals), "Medium coals" (grill 5 to 6 inches from coals) and "Medium-low coals" (grill 6 or more inches from coals). (See Grill Cooking for details.)

GRILL COOKING: Steaks, hamburgers and most quick-grilled foods require a cooking temperature of 350 to 380°F. This is accomplished by placing fully ignited briquets over prepared fire bowl base about ¾ths of an inch to 1 inch apart. This is termed a "hot fire" or "hot coals." They will burn at a high heat for 30 to 40 minutes without replenishment. Extra hot-burning briquets should be placed a little farther apart. Use a grill thermometer or hold your hand at the grilling level as a test — you should not be able to leave it there more than 3 seconds if coals are correct.

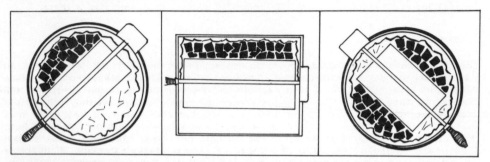

Drip pan and briquet placement for brazier bowl, square firepan, spherical cooker.

SPIT COOKING & COVERED UNIT TEMPERATURES: Most spit cooking is done at 325°F. (see inside back cover chart) and controlled by placement and replenishment of fuel (see Spit Cooking). In a covered unit, or barrel, it may be measured by an oven thermometer placed within the unit. Deluxe units generally come with a hood thermometer. Contrary to common belief, heat control in spit cooking is not determined by distance from coals on a hooded or covered unit, even though most units come with several spit-height adjustments. The heat is directly controlled by the size of the fuel layer at the back edge of the fire bowl. Raising the spit and motor for less heat, as is generally done, only results in higher heat, as the top of the hood or cover holds in the rising heat. Always leave spit at center position and adjust heat by adding or removing coals, for both open and closed spit cooking.

Barbecue Heat Control

The expert barbecue cook uses heat control, just like the kitchen range cook, to insure proper cooking and timing of recipes. Actually, charcoal cooking affords far more temperature control than most beginners realize. A grill can be controlled to cook at temperatures from "warm" to "very hot" — spit-cooking units and covered equipment can be controlled to within a few degrees of an exact roasting temperature, all through fuel selection, quantity, placement, distance, draft and reflection.

VENTS & DRAFT: Since charcoal briquets require adequate oxygen to burn, temperatures are easily controlled on covered or barrel units by opening and closing adjustable dampers at top and bottom. The more air that passes through the charcoal, from bottom to top, the hotter the temperature will be. Open vents for more heat — close down to reduce heat, using oven thermometer as a guide. Cover may also me opened slightly for additional draft.

TAP THE ASHES OFF: Charcoal cooking is a combination of direct heat and infra-red rays coming in contact with the food. As the charcoal burns, a soft gray ash appears on the surface. This ash both insulates the briquet, and prevents the rays from being released. Tap briquets with a fire rake or poker every 5 or 10 minutes to remove ash during grilling, every 20 minutes during covered cooking. Do not blow ashes off, as they will collect on food.

REFLECTION: Additional heat can be obtained through the use of foil (see Aluminum Foil In Barbecuing). A loose sheet of heavy duty foil placed "shiny side" down over grilled foods will hold in heat and reflect infra-red rays back onto the grill. Foil beneath the coals or placed within the hood also reflects heat, much as a mirror.

FOIL DRIP PAN

Whenever meats or other foods are to be cooked on a motorized spit, whether on an open brazier, barrel, wagon or covered unit, a foil drip pan should always be used. Made easily from several thicknesses of heavy-duty foil, the drip pan is placed directly on the base gravel under the spit to catch the juices and basting liquids as they roll off the meat. Clean and free of ash, these juices are collected and reused for basting or may be blended into sauces or gravy for table use. A properly used drip pan also will keep your barbecue unit clean, as juices do not fall onto hot coals, spatter or cause smoke. Gravel base materials also last longer, freed from excess grease saturation. If drippings are not to be used they are easily discarded, along with the pan when cooled.

MAKING A FOIL DRIP PAN: First, determine how large a pan you need by measuring the product to be spit-cooked. If it is a rolled roast 4 inches in diameter and a foot long, your pan should be at least 5 inches by 14 inches. This allows for a 2-inch overlap at each end, and an inch extra in width to be sure to catch all juices which drop. As pictured, pull out enough foil to cover an area more than 4-times the finished pan size. Fold it in half and flatten, then in half again to make a 4-layer thickness. Fold the ends over another 2 inches for added strength and turn up all four sides about 1½-inches high. To form tight corners, pull them out into a "spout" shape—then pinch the "spout" together vertically to form a square corner and fold each flap over against one side. Some barbecue cooks use a square block of wood as a form for shaping corners. (See Spit Barbecue Cooking for exact placement.)

FOIL TRAY FOR BRIQUETS: Barrel and covered units require far fewer briquets than open units, and many cooks like to place them in a foil tray at the rear edge of the fire pan (see Covered Cooking). Make the tray just like a drip pan, only about 2-inches wide and the length of the fire pan.

UTENSILS OF FOIL: A variety of cooking utensils may be fashioned easily from two to four thicknesses of heavy-duty foil. Simple lids, covers and basting cups may be hand formed from foil for handy barbecue use.

Barbecue Cooking Methods

All barbecue cooking falls into four general categories, Grilling, Kebobs, Spit Roasting and Covered Cooking. A basic understanding of these methods will make selection of recipes, foods, equipment and timing more meaningful to the barbecue beginner, as each has a special job to do. While many foods may be barbecued by all four methods, others are better suited to just one or two. Knowing which cooking method is best for the food and occasion is the secret to success.

GRILL COOKING

Grilling is the most popularly used barbecue method. It is best for quick-cooked foods such as steaks, chops, hamburgers, sausages, chicken pieces and small fish. Virtually all barbecue equipment is designed to grill, utilizing a flat-rod grill surface which can be placed just above the coals for intense heat. All that is required is a bed of hot charcoal briquets, tongs and steaks or "what-have-you."

TIPS: Always grease your grill before cooking with the same oil that is used on the food — if olive oil is rubbed on chicken pieces, use olive oil on the grill, etc. Space briquets evenly below grill (see Fire Building & Heat Control chapters) and control cooking temperature by raising or lowering grill. While most grilled foods are those which are to be seared and quick-cooked, others may be grill cooked for longer periods of time with the grill at it's highest position for a slower "grill-roasted" result. A sheet of heavy duty foil may be placed loosely over the food to trap in heat and flavorful fumes. This also will help hold in moisture, as does regular turning and basting. The most important thing to remember in grill cooking is to control the heat properly (see Temperature Control Heat Control) — and to be able to attain a balance between heat and cooking time which will allow the grilled food to be cooked to the desired degree of doneness without overcooking the outside. Follow recipe directions carefully.

KEBOB COOKING

Adapted from the middle-eastern cooking style of threading meats and other foods on skewers and cooking over charcoal, kebob cookery has taken on a new look in America. Most quality portable units are equipped for kebob cooking, with skewers provided which fit across wind screens or holders. Basically the same as grill cooking, kebob recipes require quick cooking over intense heat with periodic turning for even browning.

TIPS: Always balance meats and other foods evenly on skewers so that they will turn easily. Don't push foods together too tightly – let the heat get in between each piece for better cooking. Baste with marinades and basting sauces as well as season coals (see recipes) for added flavor. If unit is not equipped for kebob cookery, obtain skewers sperarately and place directly on oiled grill for easy handling. Delicate foods should always be skewer-cooked on the grill for added support. Use variety—make up new combinations. It's the real fun of kebob barbecuing!

SPIT ROASTING

Barbecuing foods on a motorized spit is also a rewarding and popular method of charcoal cooking. Most full sized units and deluxe units (including the covered models) incorporate rotisserie equipment. This method allows the barbecue cook to prepare a wide variety of foods which take even temperature cooking, much the same as oven roasting. The benefits are distinguished by the special flavoring afforded foods over charcoal and the convenient use of basting sauces or self basting (as foods turn their juices run constantly over the surface).

TIPS: Three important factors are involved in successful spit cooking. The proper fire should be prepared (see Fire Building and Heat Control chapters) and placed in an even row at the back of the fire bowl to produce a constant temperature of 325°F., and maintained for the duration of the cooking. Next, the food to be cooked, whether a rolled beef or lamb roast, spareribs or poultry, should be securely fixed on the spit rod and held in place with the spit forks and cord, if necessary. Spit forks should always be tightened with pliers then the entire spit should be picked up by the ends and rotated for balance. Any correction should be made by re-centering the food on the spit for even rotation. Finally, a drip pan should be used to catch juices, to prevent smoking and flare-up, as well as save the juice for basting and sauces.

COVERED COOKING

This is the "gourmet" barbecue cook's favorite method! Everything that can be cooked on an open unit may be barbecued on a covered unit. The differences are important to remember, however, since they effect the three basic rules of cooking time, fuel and flavoring. Unlike open cooking, covered barbecue cooking is just what the name implies — the food is cooked over the same charcoal briquets, but with a tight lid or hood covering the entire cooking procedure. Cold air is brought in through vents in the bottom of the unit, heated and released through vents in the lid. Heat is controlled by opening and closing the vents to allow more air in for hotter cooking, less for slower cooking. The air passes over and under the briquets to keep them burning, then up and around the food for cooking and flavoring. This is especially important in flavoring meats with Hickory

17

Chips & Garlic Buds (see recipe), as the fumes are concentrated around the meat more efficiently. The flavoring which results can be obtained in no other way, and, with less evaporation and more even cooking.

TIPS: Foods may be grill cooked, spit roasted or kebob barbecued on covered units. The internal temperature should be maintained at 325°F. (by adding or removing fuel and vent control) and cooking times reduced by about 20% from open cooking recipes. Little or no basting is required for most spit roasted recipes, though if marinades or cooking sauces are used, baste occasionally. Tap coals every 15 or 20 minutes for best heating regulation. Far fewer briquets are required as the heat is trapped around the food — often a dozen or less briquets will cook an entire meal. Many covered units have electric charcoal starting units built into the hood. These coils may be left on during covered cooking for additional cooking heat. Just a few briquets are then required for flavor. Cooking procedures otherwise are the same. Steaks require turning just once, as do flat roasts such as chuck, etc., for even browning. Large round roasts and poultry may be cooked directly on the grill or by using a spit. Many premium covered units also will accomodate spit baskets and other accessories.

BARBECUE MENU COMPLEMENTS

In planning any meal, the cook must select entrees which are flavor complements. The "lady of the house" knows this well, but the beginner at the barbecue unit may have some learning ahead. Plan a barbecue menu just like any special dinner. There should be a "star attraction" — which is the barbecued meat, poultry or seafood. A tangy crisp salad is always a complement, especially if the meat may be rich or greasy. The vinegar-type dressing is best, not the oily or creamy varieties. Beans and potatoes both go well with steak, but not with each other. Choose one or the other. Sweet potatoes are more flavorful than white potatoes, with ham and pork, either is fine with lamb and poultry. A green or yellow vegetable should be considered for a balanced menu. Marinades and basting sauces are also involved in the flavor contrasts of a meal. If the main dish has a spicy sauce or extra rich flavor, the other foods should be lightly seasoned for balance. Use your imagination and think your menu out carefully. It will be the difference between "just good" and "great" barbecue cooking.

TIMING YOUR BARBECUE

An expert barbecue cook will plan his cooking routine so that he can prepare a variety of foods over the same coals to complete a tasty and complete patio menu. As an example, his meat course is Spit Barbecued Whole Chicken. He also will serve Foil Baked Potatoes and a frozen green vegetable, both to be cooked with the same coals, along with the chicken. To have them all get done at the same time is the secret to barbecue success. It's easy to do, even for the beginner, if the recipes are followed. Each recipe will tell cooking time. Just figure the individual times back from the serving time, and place the food on the grill or among the coals as their respective requirements come up. Say the chickens take 1¼ hours — start them off. The frozen vegetables will take 50 minutes, wrapped in foil on the coals and the potatoes 40 minutes (see recipes). When the chicken has cooked 35 minutes, start the vegetables, the the potatoes 10 minutes later. All should be done at the same time. Some units have warming ovens and if the main course takes longer than expected, set vegetable and potatoes in to keep warm, or at a spot away from the coals in the fire pan. Use this procedure for breads, cooked garnishes and desserts.

Barbecue Seasoning

MARINADES, BASTING SAUCES & GLAZES

Marinades and cooking sauces have four important functions in barbecue cooking. They flavor, tenderize, color and impart juices to the food. Many of the recipes in this book do all of these culinary aids, while others are for specialized purposes or flavors. The individual recipe names and text should make identification and use an easy and challenging undertaking. Marinades and basting sauces have three primary ingredients, oil, seasoning and acidity. The oil keeps the cooking food from drying out over the heat from open coals. The seasoning imparts the desired flavor, and the acid (vinegar, citrus juice or wine) both flavors and tenderizes (see Tenderizers). Marinades are used first as a tenderizing and flavoring agent for meats, poultry and some seafoods. The entree is placed in the marinade liquid for several hours or overnight to allow the flavors to be properly absorbed and for the tenderizing to take place. Then the liquid may be used again as a cooking or basting sauce. Cooking sauces are those which are brushed or spooned over the meat, poultry or seafood while it cooks — generally on a spit or grill. Glazes are those cooking sauces which produce a special outside coating on cooked foods, combining flavor with color. They are usually brushed on during the final minutes of cooking to prevent burning, as in the case of Orange Glaze for pork — which contains sugar and fruit juice. Both would burn if brushed on too soon.

TIPS: Select marinades and cooking sauces with care — they are meant to enhance the flavor of the food, not disguise or change it! Be sure to select marinades and sauces which are flavor complements to the food to be cooked — a sauce which is excellent with pork may not be correct for beef or veal. A general rule of success is to use oily marinades and cooking sauces on dry or lean foods, non-oily (vinegar & wine base) sauces on oily or high fat foods. If additional color is desired for food, select a basting sauce with soy sauce for brown, fruit juice or pureed-fruit for delicate coloring. It is very important to remember not to use sauces which contain tomato products as a cooking or basting sauce. The tomato will burn to a black crusty coating before the food is cooked, in most cases. If tomato flavoring (commercial barbecue sauce types) is desired, baste these sauces on only during the final few minutes of cooking to prevent burning.

BARBECUE TABLE SAUCES

Table and sandwich sauces should not be confused with marinades and cooking sauces (see Marinades, Basting Sauces & Glazes) as most contain tomato and will burn during cooking. Several table sauce recipes are included which are made for seasoning cooked meats, poultry and seafood, for serving and in sandwiches. These are the popular "spicy" or "western" variety and should not be used in quantities which cover up the rich natural flavor of the barbecued entree. Commercial brands are fine, if used in moderation. A good trick is to blend natural meat drippings (from the drip pan) with the table sauce and serve warm for a rich and "genuine" barbeque meat flavor. If your barbecued entree was properly charcoal cooked, according to the recipe, chances are that it really doesn't need any further seasoning. Try a taste first, before sloshing on the table sauce.

Selecting Meats For Barbecuing

While most barbecue enthusiasts regularly enjoy the traditional favorites, such as steaks, chops, ribs, ground meat and kebob cubes, it should be remembered that a great many other meat cuts also are excellent for barbecuing. In fact, any meat cut which may be pan-fried, broiled, grilled or dry roasted is suitable for charcoal cooking. As the recipes in this book will indicate, some of the best barbecued meat courses are to be found in large roasts, spit-roasted to perfection. More economical beef cuts, such as chuck and flank steaks, short ribs and others, can be festive barbecue fare. Lamb, a gourmet favorite among barbecue experts, can open a whole new world of barbecue variety to the beginner. Just try lamb ribs in place of pork next time for a surprising switch in spareribs! Or mix them in a spit basket with beef and pork ribs for a blend of flavors. Barbecue enjoyment begins with selecting the correct meat — not just the same familiar cuts over again, and not just for price. Here are some general pointers on buying meats for barbecuing — and if in doubt about any cut, or have any questions, be sure to ask your butcher. He will be more than happy to help, especially when special cuts or preparation are involved. Some of the recipes in this book call for special trim, rolling and tieing of meats which your butcher can do best. Be sure to tell him it's for barbecuing, and whether for grill, spit or covered cooking. He will know what to do. He also will help you to learn more about meat cuts, names and their cooking application.

TENDERIZERS

A number of commercial meat tenderizers are available in markets and can be very useful in barbecue cooking of less-tender cuts of meats. Use according to package directions. Excess use or prolonged periods of tenderizing before cooking will result in "mushy," undesirable meat. Wines, vinegar and citrus juices also act as tenderizers when used in marinades (see recipes).

PORTIONS

Outdoor appetites tend to be bigger than indoor ones, and it may be that the fresh air, savory aromas and fun of barbecue cooking will stimulate the taste buds even more than you think. Here are some basic rules for portion figuring which will help at the market ahead of time and insure that appetites will be satisfied.

TIPS: For steaks and chops, plan on ½ to ¾ lb. of boneless steak per serving — 1 lb. for big appetites. Bone-in steaks, ¾ to 1½ lbs. per serving. Rolled boneless roasts, ½ to ¾ lb. per person. Bone in roasts (rib of beef), ¾ to 1¼ lb. per serving. Chickens (2 to 3 lb. size), ½ chicken per serving. Ribs, meaty, 1 to 1½ lbs. per serving, spare, 1½ to 2 lbs. per serving. Whole turkeys should be figured at ¼ to ½ lb. per serving. All weights are uncooked. Better to have leftovers than run short!

BEEF

TIPS: The best cuts of beef for barbecuing are from the loin section, including the prime steaks, whole tenderloin, rib roast and short ribs. Adjoining this section is the chuck, a good barbecue cut. Rump and sirloin roasts may be spit roasted, though best when rolled and larded. Ground meat should be fairly lean to avoid excessive fat dripping. Always select steaks which are well shaped and marbled with fine lines of fat. Excessive fat should be trimmed from edges, leaving only enough for flavor (see Basic Grilled Steaks recipe). Well aged steaks will have a dull red color and the fat should be firm and white. Thick steak cuts, from 1 to 2 inches are best for barbecuing. (See recipes for details.) Buy beef no more than one or two days before cooking, ground beef the same day if possible. Frozen beef should be thawed before barbecuing (see Barbecuing From The Freezer chapter).

LAMB

TIPS: Lamb should always be young and tender (now available all year long). More tender than beef, most lamb cuts are well suited for barbecue. Besides the popular chops, leg roast and shoulder, try lamb ribs (breast), ground lamb and leg steaks. Lamb is at it's best using any of the marinades suggested in recipes and cooked with the delicate flavors of hickory smoke and charcoal.

PORK

TIPS: Pork should be selected with a keen eye towards the amount of fat on the cut. Most pork cuts are suitable for barbecuing, especially chops, ribs, loins, legs and shoulders. Since the fat is what causes excess dripping and sometimes flareups, as much of the heavy fat as possible should be trimmed away prior to cooking. Use a drip pan for roasts (see Drip Pan chapter) and consider the use of marinades and basting sauces for variety (see recipes). Pork should always be cooked well-done, according to recipe directions or meat thermometer readings listed.

VEAL

TIPS: Being young beef, veal will be less fat-marbled than beef and also have less outside fat. Select the same cuts as for beef. Some barbecue cooks like to combine veal with other meats, such as pork or lamb, in combination kebobs and rolled roasts. It generally is cooked more well done than beef.

SAUSAGES

TIPS: Most sausages are entertaining treats when barbecue cooked. Grilled or spit roasted, the charcoal flavor enhances the spiced or smoked flavors of sausages. Care should be taken to see that uncooked varieties are cooked through, and that excess fat dripping does not cause flareup. A good trick is to keep them moving on the grill with tongs so that they don't drip in the same place. A good variety of sausages makes a swell barbecue hors d' oeuvre — let the guests do it themselves with skewers. Also, a number-one barbecue favorite with children, see Hot Dog Bonanza recipes.

SPECIALTY MEATS

TIPS: Barbecue cooking may be the secret to more popular acceptance of such nutritious foods as liver, heart, sweetbreads and kidneys.

POULTRY

TIPS: Almost all poultry may be barbecued (with the exception of stewing chickens) and should be selected for size, according to portions required. (See Portions.) Young fryer chickens may be barbecued in a variety of ways, as can ducks, geese, cornish hens and game (see recipes). Turkeys should be of the "broad-breasted" variety, not more than 18 lbs. A variety of poultry marinades and basting sauces are included in the recipes. Always cook poultry completely, according to recipe directions or meat thermometer readings listed.

FISH & SEAFOOD

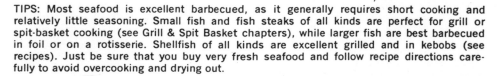

TIPS: Most seafood is excellent barbecued, as it generally requires short cooking and relatively little seasoning. Small fish and fish steaks of all kinds are perfect for grill or spit-basket cooking (see Grill & Spit Basket chapters), while larger fish are best barbecued in foil or on a rotisserie. Shellfish of all kinds are excellent grilled and in kebobs (see recipes). Just be sure that you buy very fresh seafood and follow recipe directions carefully to avoid overcooking and drying out.

BEANS, STEWS & CASSEROLES

TIPS: Beans are as much a part of a barbecue menu as the checkered table cloth — at least to many patio chefs. While your barbecue unit can't cook the beans from scratch, it certainly can impart individuality to prepared varieties. Several recipes for beans are included, all to be heated on the grill or in a covered unit. A variety of additional seasonings may be added to canned beans, including meats, fruits and spices. They are further "seasoned" with the rich flavor of the buring charcoal and hickory chips. Here is another place to develop individual "bean specialities." Several stew and casserole dishes may also be heated in the same way as well as in foil packages. This is especially good for canned hash, chili bean mixtures and stews (see recipes). On larger units, the beans or casserole entrees may be prepared right on the grill at the same time that the course is cooking. Any oven-proof container may be used on a grill or in a covered unit. Even a frying pan may be used to heat beans, lightly covered with foil.

VEGETABLES

TIPS: While barbecue cooking has always been a favorite way to cook potatoes and corn, it also can do wonders for many leafy greens, squash, tomatoes and other fresh vegetables. Most frozen vegetables may also be cooked in foil over charcoal (see recipes). The recipe section has all the old favorites, corn & potatoes in foil, etc., but there are several really new ideas, for both entree and garnish. Start with Vegetable Kebobs (see recipe), and cook your whole patio menu right on the barbecue!

FRUITS

TIPS: Fruits long have been used as barbecue garnish — grilled pineapple slices, apples and citrus fruits. By using the new techniques of foil cookery (see recipes), tasty new fruit dishes are easily cooked over charcoal to be used as entrees, desserts and children's specialties. Try the recipes suggested, then improvise on your own — there are untold new combinations of fruit and flavoring dishes yet to be discovered!

BREADS & BAKING

TIPS: Barbecue units were not designed for actual bread baking, but such campfire favorites as biscuits and shortbread can be cooked over charcoal. Generally, bread entrees, such as Garlic French Bread or Cheese Bread (see recipes), are warmed on the grill or in a warming oven during the last minutes of cooking. A special barbecue flavor can be imparted to warmed breads by opening the foil wrapper a little before removing from the grill to allow the charcoal fumes to penetrate the slices.

SANDWICHES

TIPS: With the exception of barbecued hamburgers, hot dogs and steak sandwiches, barbecued sandwiches, as we know them in America, seldom are really true barbecue fare. Usually they are made up of re-warmed cooked meat (often not barbecued at all) which is blended with a spicy tomato sauce and served in a bun or French roll. Real barbecue sandwiches require barbecued meat, poultry or seafood, freshly cooked and seasoned, if desired, with sauce. They are so much more delicious than the "mock" variety that you probably will never again call them "barbecue sandwiches" away from your grill (See Genuine Barbecue Sandwiches recipe.)

SEASONING THE COALS

Additional flavoring can be imparted to open and closed barbecue recipes by tossing a variety of seasonings onto the coals during cooking (see Hickory Chips & Garlic Buds recipe). Some of these seasonings are, onion and garlic salt, bay leaves and other leafy herbs, onion and garlic pieces, pepper corns and most fruit wood chips, such as apple and citrus wood. Do not use soft wood chips.

COOKING WITH WINES & SPIRITS

Dry table wine is an excellent barbecue marinade and sauce ingredient as it has exceptional tenderizing qualities when used with meats. It also imparts delicate flavoring, along with distilled spirits. In every case, the alcohol content is completely removed through evaporation during cooking, leaving only the flavor. These recipes are perfectly suitable for the whole family. As a substitute for wines and spirits in recipes, use apple juice, fruit juices and bouillon, if desired.

USE A MEAT THERMOMETER

The only really sure way to determine the exact doneness of a barbecued roast is to use a meat thermometer. Always select the all-metal variety, with a round dial top, for easy reading. Insert the thermometer into the thickest part of the meat or poultry, being sure not to touch any bone or the metal spit. Use for grilling, spit roasting and covered cooking barbecue methods. Follow chart instructions (inside back cover) for times and temperatures. Thermometer may be left in meat throughout cooking.

CARVING & SERVING

TIPS: Large meat roasts and poultry require carving prior to serving. While some barbecue buffs prefer to serve meats in "rugged" cuts, the expert will carve his entree as correctly as possible for attractive servings and easy portion control. A large carving board is suggested (with a capacity to collect juices) as well as a good, sharp carving set. Both meats and poultry should be allowed to "set" in a warm place for from 15 to 20 minutes after cooking and before carving, to let the meat and juices "firm up" properly. This will make carving easier and retain a maximum of juice in the food. Carving can be done at the table or at the barbecue unit, with servings dished up individually or placed on a platter. Added flavor can be imparted to sliced meats by pouring over fat-skimmed natural meat cooking juices or warmed sauces at serving time. Be sure to garnish. The accompanying photos show basic carving techniques for popular cuts of meats. The most important thing is to do your carving quickly and efficiently so that the meal is served hot!

Carving techniques for Rib Roast, Leg Of Lamb and Ham are pictured.

GARNISH & EYE-APPEAL

TIPS: Barbecue cooking of meats, poultry and seafood is probably the most colorful method of any. Foods take on a rich, outdoor-roasted look which is even brighter and more appealing in sunlight. To make the picture complete, the expert barbecue cook will take full advantage of garnish — the dressing up of his entree at serving time to make the colors even more eye-appealing. It takes only a second to spot a sprig or two of fresh green parsley or a red tomato wedge beside the cooked barbecued course, and what a difference it makes! A number of garnish recipes are included which will give dishes a real "gourmet" look, such as Grilled Pineapple Slices, Vegetable and Fruit Kebobs (see recipes). Glazes and basting sauces also add color to foods. Just be sure the flavors are complementary. Other popular garnishes are: paprika, course pepper, parsley flakes, lemon wedges, stuffed olives, pearl onions, beets, spiced crab apples or peaches, green pepper slices, carrot sticks or curls, hard-cooked eggs, lettuce, radishes, pickles, water cress, mushrooms — "and what-have-you."

LEFTOVERS

Barbecue leftovers can be a real treat. They may be frozen, wrapped in foil and rewarmed in a moderate oven. A popular favorite with the children is to put leftover barbecue meats, vegetables and sauce in saved frozen dinner trays, cover with foil and freeze your own "quick barbecue dinners." Reheat in the standard way. Fresh leftover meats are easily heated in a moderate oven with additional sauce added for moisture. Lean pieces of meat and poultry should be sliced thin for use in barbecue sandwiches (see recipe). In every case, the flavor of the charcoal cooking is retained for many more days of enjoyment!

Barbecuing From The Freezer

Economical buying and superior cooking results have made barbecuing of frozen foods very popular. For meats, especially, barbecue cooking is far superior to kitchen preparation as the "quick searing" offered by charcoal heat seals the meat immediately, retaining a maximum of juices. Many barbecue experts have meat cut especially for charcoal cooking when ordering freezer meat. The steaks should be cut 1½ inches or more thick and roasts rolled and larded in even width rolls, etc. Poultry, seafoods and other barbecue favorites can be sized according to recipe requirements prior to freezing for convenience.

TIPS: In most cases, meats should be completely thawed before cooking. Exceptions are thin steaks and chops which may be grilled frozen, figuring extra cooking time (see recipes). To avoid excess juice loss, meats may be started as soon as soft throughout — warming to room temperature not necessary. Use meat thermometer. A rich oil basting sauce will help seal surfaces quickly. Frozen meats may be used exactly as fresh in all recipes, with marinades, glazes and seasonings. Frozen vegetables may be cooked in foil (see recipe), as well as thawed — by shortening cooking time. Frozen meats should be used within six months for prime flavor.

Graduation Time

Congratulations! You have just completed the BARBECUE COLLEGE COURSE. With the basic information which you have covered, you are now in position to try and successfully prepare any of the recipes which follow. There is no better way to celebrate than to go out and cook up a feast. And, as an added bonus, you are now entitled to become a BARBECUE COLLEGE graduate, by completing the Examination Form, located just inside the back cover. Answer all of the questions and Chef Bell will grade them and award each passing student with an official diploma, enscribed with his or her name, and decreeing upon the graduate, the honorary degree of Master of Barbecuing. Thousands of Americans already have earned this honor and proudly display their diplomas in kitchen, patio or den. (See instructions on form.) And "Happy Barbecuing" to you and your family. Sincerely,

Ed Bell.

MEATS

Informal mealtime setting features succulent barbecued rolled roast.

QUICK KEY TO BARBECUE MEAT VARIETY

Each recipe title in the Meat Chapter is accompanied by one or more of the above symbols. They denote the variety of meats which may be used with the recipe, for easy and immediate identification. The symbols, for beef, lamb and pork, appear in a sequence which shows the most popularly used meat closest to the recipe title. The following symbols are recommended alternatives. Check recipes for possible changes in cooking times, handling and seasonings between meat varieties.

25

Steaks

BASIC GRILLED STEAKS

SELECTION:

Always select top-quality steaks, well marbeled with fat and in the "tender cuts" catagory (see meats chapter). These include, Fillet, Tenderloin, Top Sirloin, New York, Delmonico, Spencer, T-bone, Porterhouse, Rib and Club steak cuts.

PORTIONS:

For uncooked boneless steak, well trimmed of fat, plan on at least ½ to ¾ lb. per serving — or more for big appetites. For bone-in steaks, plan on ¾ to 1¼ lbs. per serving. A single 1 inch thick Club or Rib steak will provide a generous serving for one person, while larger cuts, such as Top Sirloin and Porterhouse, can serve two to four, depending on thickness. Many popular barbecue steak dishes, such as Chateaubriands or Gaucho Thick Steak (see recipes), will serve up to six from a single cut of Top Sirloin.

PREPARATION:

Generally, steaks should be removed from the refrigerator an hour or more before cooking and allowed to warm to room temperature. This assures even cooking and reliable estimating of cooking times. Exceptions are thin frozen steaks, which may be quick grilled unthawed to retain juices. See Barbecuing From The Freezer section.

Slash the edges of fat in several places to keep meat from curling during barbecuing. Brush or rub steaks lightly with salad oil, olive oil, melted butter or margarine before grilling. Steaks may be marinated before cooking (see marinade recipes). If only salt and pepper is desired, season only during the last minutes of cooking or when serving. Salt tends to draw the moisture out of steaks if applied before cooking.

GRILLING:

Place steaks on an oiled grill 3 to 4 inches above prepared coals. Take care to see that juices stay in by never turning steaks with a fork or sharp object. Always use tongs so that the meat will not be punctured. Steaks should never be turned more than once, unless called for in a specific recipe. Juices will be lost and steaks toughened through unnecessary turning.

For seared steaks, lower grill to 3 inches above coals during first minute or two of cooking, raising to 5 inches until ready to turn. Then lower grill again and repeat searing and raise grill for finishing. This is an excellent method for rare and medium rare cooking. Medium to well done steaks are best grilled higher off the coals and for longer periods of time to avoid excessive searing.

BASIC GRILLING TIMES:

Check for doneness by cutting near bone or at the thickest part of the outer edge of meat and noting color. Rare will be bright red, medium, red to pink, and well, pink to gray.
A 1-inch thick steak, grilled 3 to 5 inches from coals (with or without searing procedure) will cook in the following approximate times:
RARE — 2½ to 3 minutes per side
MEDIUM — 3 to 5 minutes per side
WELL — 5 to 6 minutes per side

For thicker steaks, add 2 minutes per ½-inch of additional thickness to the above schedule. (Times will vary with the fuel — some briquets burn hotter than others. See Fuels & Fire Starting section.)

SERVING:

Always serve steaks immediately — hot off the grill! Steaks will lose juice and toughen if allowed to stand or cool before serving. Garnish with parsley, Vegetable Kebobs, Grilled Onion Rings, Mushroom Kebobs, Sauces or Relishes of your choice (see recipes).

GRILLED STEAK & MUSHROOMS

Select top quality steak, Tenderloin, Top Sirloin, Spencer, New York, T-bone, Porterhouse, etc., and grill according to Basic Grilled Steaks (see recipe). Serve topped with Mushroom Steak Sauce (see recipe) and garnish with parsley sprigs, Vegetable Kebobs (see recipe), pototoes or beans.

GRILLED GARLIC STEAK

Select and prepare steak according to Basic Grilled Steaks (see recipe). Just before grilling, rub all meat surfaces of steak with cut fresh garlic cloves, or lightly sprinkle with garlic powder. Rub lightly with oil and grill to desired doneness. Serve topped with a pat of Garlic Butter (see recipe).

BOURBON TOP SIRLOIN

Sprinkle a thick top sirloin steak with ¼ cup bourbon, and allow to stand at room temperature about 2 hours. Turn occasionally adding bourbon as needed. Barbecue steak according to Basic Grilled Steaks (see recipe). During cooking, spirits from the bourbon burn off completely, leaving only a delicate flavor which will require only salt and pepper be added just before serving.

SALT-CRUSTED SIRLOIN

Have top sirloin steak cut from 1½ to 2-inches thick, and weighing from 3 to 4 lbs. Mix 1 to 1½ cups salt with enough water to make a thick paste and spread on steak, coating it entirely with about ¼-inch layer. Place on grill 3-inches over hot coals and cook 8 to 12 minutes on each side, depending on doneness desired. The salt will form a hard black crust during cooking, holding all of the meat juices in the steak. Remove crust by cracking with a hammer and discard. Place steak on a deep pre-warmed platter and pour ½ cup melted butter, or seasoned butter (see recipes) over meat before slicing in diagonal cuts. Serve meat on toasted slices of French bread topped with natural juice and a butter mixture.

ROQUEFORT NEW YORK STEAK

Grill thick New York steaks according to Basic Grilled Steaks (see recipe) to desired doneness. Remove to hot platter and quickly sprinkle with crumbled Roquefort cheese, or spread with a mixture of 1 part melted butter to three parts Roquefort. Allow the cheese mixture to melt a few seconds before serving. Season lightly with salt and fresh ground pepper. Garnish with parsley or Vegetable Kebobs (see recipe).

VARIATIONS: Use Bleu, Stilton or Gorgonzola cheese in place of Roquefort, and any cut of tender steak.

CHARRED STEAK SPECTACULAR

For a spectacular change in steak barbecuing, build a bed of hot coals at least 2 or 3 layers deep, and twice the size of the steaks to be cooked. When burning uniformly, tap and blow off as much ash as possible from the tops of coals. Then toss unseasoned steaks (1½-inch) directly onto coals. Char 3 to 5 minutes, depending on desired doneness, and turn with tongs onto fresh coals. Remove to cutting board and scrape away excess crust. Slice diagonally and serve with sauce or seasoned only with salt, pepper and butter.

PEPPER STEAK

3 lbs. sirloin steak, 1½-inches thick
1 to 2 tbs. cracked fresh black peppercorns

1 tsp. salt or to taste
¼ cup brandy (optional)
¼ cup butter, melted

Press cracked peppercorns into both sides of steak. Let the steak stand 20 to 30 minutes. Place on greased grill about 3 to 4-inches from hot coals and cook 3 to 7 minutes on each side, depending upon how rare you want the steak. Season with salt. Remove steak to platter and pour over warmed brandy and ignite. When flame dies, pour over melted butter and serve at once.

CHATEAUBRIAND

Have the butcher cut top sirloin about 2 to 3-inches thick. Brush it with butter or olive oil, and place on grill, very close to hot coals; sear about 3 minutes on each side. Raise grill to 5-inches and cook about 10 to 18 minutes on each side, depending on desired doneness. Baste several times with melted butter. Chateaubriand is traditionally served rare. Lay the meat on a hot platter and cut into diagonal slices. Season with salt and pepper. Serve immediately with additional melted or seasoned butter or Bearnaise Sauce (see recipes) poured over meat.

TOURNEDOS OF BEEF

Tournedos are cut from the narrow end of the beef filet, though top sirloin will do. They are usually fairly thick, from 1 to 1½-inches. Wrap a strip of bacon around edge, tying with string or securing with tooth pick. Brush meat with salad oil or butter, sprinkle with desired seasonings and place on greased grill. Barbecue over medium hot coals approximately 3 to 8 minutes on each side, depending on degree of doneness desired. Turn with tongs. Serve with desired sauce or relish; excellent topped with grilled fresh mushrooms (see recipe).

MEXICAN BEEFSTEAK

Rub about 1 pound tender beefsteak with a mixture of 1 crushed clove garlic, 2 tbs. chili powder and 2 tbs. wine vinegar. Let marinate 3 or 4 hours at room temperature. If steak is very lean, brush with a little oil and place on grill. Cook over coals according to desired doneness, (See Basic Grilled Steaks), turning once. Salt just before serving. Serve with Mexican Salsa Relish (see recipe).

BUTTER CHUCK STEAK

I large chuck steak, 1 to
 2-inches thick
Unseasoned meat
 tenderizer

¼ cup butter, melted
Salt and pepper to taste

Place steak in shallow pan and tenderize according to directions on meat tenderizer package. Let stand at room temperature 20 to 30 minutes before brushing with butter. Place meat on hot grill and barbecue 5 to 10 minutes on each side, depending on degree of doneness desired. Brush often with melted butter, season with salt and pepper to taste just before serving.

CHEF'S GRILLED STEAK

3 to 4 lbs. steak, 1-inch
 thick
½ cup salad oil
2 tbs. lemon juice
⅛ tsp. instant garlic
 powder

1 tsp. onion salt
½ tsp. Worcestershire
 sauce
½ tsp. seasoned salt

Make marinade by combining seasoning ingredients in jar and shake well. Coat steak with marinade and place in shallow pan in remaining marinade for several hours, turning occasionally. Cook about 3-inches over hot coals for 2 to 10 minutes on each side, or until steak has reached desired degree of doneness. A rare steak will cook in about 2 to 3 minutes on each side.

GAUCHO THICK STEAK

6 lb. top sirloin steak,
 3-inches thick
¼ cup brandy
½ lb. fresh mushrooms,
 sliced

½ cup vinegar-oil or
 French dressing
Salt and pepper to taste

Marinate steak in brandy, turning often, about 30 minutes to 1 hour. Place mushrooms in shallow bowl and marinate in remaining ingredients at least for 1 hour. Place steaks on greased grill 4 to 6-inches from hot coals. Barbecue taking care not to char bottom before turning. When juices appear on top sides of steaks, turn with tongs, season with salt and pepper and continue grilling until desired degree of doneness (from 8 to 15 minutes on each side). Remove steaks to heated-platter and slice into ½-inch diagonal pieces. Pour over mushrooms, and serve immediately.

PARISIAN CHOPPED STEAK

Crumble 3 ozs. roquefort or blue cheese into 1 lb. chopped beef or ground beef. Add 3 tbs. finely minced green onion tops; mix well and pat into 1-inch thick oval. Place on greased grill 4 to 5-inches above hot coals and cook 5 to 8 minutes per side or to desired doneness. Season with salt and freshly ground black pepper to taste.

JUICY CHOPPED STEAK

Mix 1 lb. chopped steak or ground beef with ¼ cup evaporated milk. Lightly season with salt, pepper, monosodium glutamate and a dash of garlic powder (optional). Pat into a 1-inch thick oval and place on greased grill 4 to 5-inches obove medium-hot coals. Grill 5 to 7 minutes on each side, or to desired doneness. If meat is very lean, brush with a little oil or melted butter while cooking. Garnish with watercress.

SALISBURY STEAK

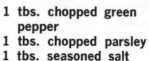

1½ lbs. ground beef	1 tbs. chopped green
1 lb. ground lamb or	pepper
lean pork (or both)	1 tbs. chopped parsley
6 strips bacon, partially	1 tbs. seasoned salt
cooked	¼ tbs. pepper
2 tbs. chopped onion	

Chop bacon and blend with meat, vegetables and seasonings. Shape into large serving-size patties and grill over medium coals 5 to 8 minutes per side, or to desired doneness. Serve with vegetable relishes; no sauce generally required. (Note: If pork is used, cook to well done — meat proportions may be adjusted to taste as long as 2½ lbs. is total.)

LUAU CHOPPED STEAK

1 lb. chopped ground	1 9-oz. can pineapple
beef or lamb	slices
¼ tsp. salt	½ cup catsup
1 tsp. soy sauce	¼ cup brown sugar
Dash of pepper	2 tsp. Worcestershire

Drain pineapple, saving about 2 tbs. juice. Season meat with salt, pepper and soy, and shape into thick patties. Press a pineapple slice firmly into each patty, sealing around edges of slice so it won't fall out during cooking. Make a sauce of pineapple juice, catsup, brown sugar and Worcestershire heated together. Brush on patties, and broil over hot coals about 12 minutes or until

meat is done and pineapple nicely glazed. Brush often during cooking with sauce. Serve with grilled fruit garnish (see recipes).

GRILLED MINUTE STEAK

4 ¼ to ½-inch thick
   minute steaks
½ cup butter or
   margarine, melted
1 tbs. lemon juice

2 tbs. parsley, minced
1 tbs. chives, minced
Salt and pepper
Toasted buns

Mix the butter, lemon juice, parsley and chives together and coat steaks. Place on grill about 3-inches above hot coals and cook about 2 minutes on each side. Brush several times with butter mixture. Season with salt and pepper and serve at once on toasted buns.

FROZEN STEAK SANDWICH

Brush melted butter over frozen cube or minute steak, and place on grill 3-inches from coals. Grill 2 to 5 minutes, or until juices begin to appear on the uncooked side of meat. Turn and barbecue until done. Season with salt and freshly ground black pepper. Place on toasted buttered French bread or rolls, serve with tomato slices, lettuce and relish.

ROUND STEAK IN FOIL

2 lbs. round steak, 1-
   inch thick
¼ cup flour
1 tsp. salt
¼ tsp. pepper
1 tsp. paprika

2 tbs. bacon fat
1 cup catsup
1 medium onion, sliced
½ tsp. garlic salt
½ cup green pepper,
   chopped

Mix the flour, salt, pepper and paprika and pound into meat with mallet. Pour bacon fat in skillet on grill and quickly saute steak until browned on both sides. Combine catsup with remaining ingredients and spoon half of this mixture in center of double-thick aluminum foil; place steak on top, cover with remaining tomato mixture. Fold the foil over and seal edges (see Foil Cooking chapter). Place foil-wrapped steak over medium coals and cook 1½ hours or until meat is tender. Turn several times with tongs. Five minutes before steak is done, open top of foil to allow charcoal fumes to flavor meat. Serve steak in its own juice with vegetables as garnish.

SWISS STEAK PACKET DINNER
(Individual Serving — Cook One Recipe Per Person)

6 oz. round steak
1 tbs. flour
1 carrot, cut in strips
1 small onion, quartered
1 small potato, pared
and cut in strips
2 green pepper rings

¼ cup chopped celery
2 tbs. catsup
½ tsp. salt
Dash of pepper
1 tbs. dry red wine or
water

Pound flour into steak and place on square of double thick alumi-num foil. Arrange the vegetables on and around steak. Top with remaining ingredients. Sprinkle with wine or water. Wrap secure-ly and bake on grill 30 to 40 minutes, turning about every 10 minutes to prevent burning on bottom. Serve from foil or bowl.

GRILLED FLANK STEAK

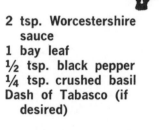

1½ lb. flank steak,
scored
⅔ cup catsup
½ cup water
⅓ cup lemon juice (or
wine vinegar)
1 tsp. celery seeds

2 tsp. Worcestershire
sauce
1 bay leaf
½ tsp. black pepper
¼ tsp. crushed basil
Dash of Tabasco (if
desired)

Combine all ingredients (except steak) and simmer uncovered for 10 minutes and cool to room temperature. Pour over flank steak in shallow pan and place in refrigerator overnight. Turn occasionally. Warm to room temperature and place about 4-inches above hot coals. Grill 5 to 7 minutes on each side. Heat marinade and serve with flank steak that has been cut in very thin slices diagonally across the grain.

LONDON BROIL

2 lbs. flank steak, 1-inch
thick
Meat tenderizer
1 clove garlic, halved

¼ cup butter, margarine
or peanut oil
Salt and pepper

Sprinkle both sides of steak with tenderizer, pierce meat deeply at 1-inch intervals. Let stand at room temperature about 1 hour. Rub both sides of steak with garlic and brush with butter or oil. Place on grill 2 to 3 inches above hot coals and cook for about 4 to 6 minutes on each side. Turn once during cooking. Remove to hot platter, season with salt and pepper and top with generous amount of butter. To serve cut in diagonal thin slices across grain.

ROLLED LONDON BROIL

Season tenderized flank steak with salt and pepper and roll up, starting at the thin end. Lard with bacon strips if desired and tie at 1-inch intervals with heavy string. With a sharp knife, cut off 1-inch steaks by slicing in between string ties. Leave the string intact to hold steaks during cooking. Brush with melted butter and grill 3-inches from coals 5 to 8 minutes on each side, or to desired doneness. Serve topped with a pat of butter, a sprinkling of paprika and chopped parsley.

SHERRIED LAMB STEAKS

2½ lbs. shoulder steaks or chops, cut 1 inch thick	½ cup olive oil, or salad oil
2 tbs. green onion, minced	1 bay leaf
	¾ tsp. basil
¼ cup tarragon wine vinegar	½ tsp. oregano
	½ tsp. black pepper
	¾ cup dry sherry wine

Place lamb steaks in shallow pan. Mix remaining ingredients together and pour over lamb; marinate 2 to 4 hours (or overnight in refrigerator), turning several times. Let meat stand at room temperature at least 1 hour before barbecuing. Drain lamb steaks well and place on grill over hot coals 20 to 35 minutes, turning with tongs frequently and basting with the marinade. Heat any remaining marinade and serve with lamb steaks.

BARBECUED PORK STEAKS

Use tenderloin pork steaks, cut 1 to 1¼-inches thick. Grease grill with pork fat and place steaks close to coals to sear, about 2½ minutes on each side. Raise grill to 6-inches and cook slowly 25 to 30 minutes, or until done, turning once. If desired, brush meat with Lemon Butter or Hot Sauce Butter (see recipes) during grilling. For hickory smoked flavor, add a few hickory chips to coals.

GRILLED HAM STEAKS

Place ham steaks, ½-inch thick, on lightly greased grill and cook until lightly browned. Turn, and continue grilling about 15 minutes more, or until heated through. If desired, brush with your favorite barbecue sauce (see recipes), or place a pineapple ring and a candied cherry on each slice after turning.

GRILLED HAM SLICE

1 slice (center cut) of
   ham, 1-inch thick
¼ tsp. cloves
1 tsp. dry mustard
¼ tsp. ginger

¼ tsp. allspice
⅓ cup brown sugar,
   firmly packed
¼ cup cider vinegar

Slash edges of fat on ham slice to prevent curling. Mix remaining ingredients and brush over ham. Grill over coals 15 minutes or until done, turning often and basting with sauce. Garnish with grilled pineapple slices (see recipe).

Chops

CHEF BELL'S PINEAPPLE-PORK CHOP BRUNCH

Cut top from a large fresh pineapple without removing ends or rind. Rinse and cut crosswise into 9 round slices. Take 8 smoked pork chops (the pre-cooked variety) and alternate on spit with pineapple slices with top and bottom of pineapple at ends. Secure with spit forks and cook over medium coals about 45 minutes. Meat thermometer inserted into pork chop should read 160°F. Season coals with Hickory Chips and Garlic Buds (see recipe) during cooking. Serve on lettuce leaves garnished with cherry or spiced fruit, each on top of a pineapple ring.

GRILLED PORK CHOPS

Use pork loin or rib chops, cut 1 to 1¼-inches thick. Place on hot grill (that has been greased with pork fat), close to coals to sear meat, about 2 to 3½ minutes each side. Raise grill to 6-inches and cook slowly 20 to 30 minutes, turning once, or until well done. During last 10 minutes of cooking, add hickory chips to coals if desired, or brush with Ginger Baste For Pork (see recipe).

PORK CHOPS IN BASKET

Lock rib or loin pork chops, cut 1 to 1¼-inches thick, into spit basket. Broil over slow coals 45 minutes to 1 hour, or until well done. During last 20 minutes, add hickory and buds of garlic to coals, and if desired, brush with your favorite barbecue sauce (see recipes).

SPIT BASKET LAMB CHOPS

Use thick center cut loin or rib lamb chops and brush with a

little melted butter, olive oil or Italian salad dressing. Place in spit basket (see Equipment section). Roast over medium hot coals about 30 minutes or until nicely browned. Season with salt and pepper, or your choice of barbecue sauce (see recipes) a few minutes before removing from heat.

FRENCH LAMB CHOPS

8 rib lamb chops, 1 to
   1½-inches thick
½ cup Lemon Butter

Salt and pepper
Heavy duty aluminum foil

French bone ends of chops (see Lamb Chart) and wrap in aluminum foil to prevent charring. Grill chops 8 to 10 minutes each side or until done. Season with salt and pepper just before serving, brush with warm Lemon Butter (see recipe).

PEACH-CURRY LAMB CHOPS

6 to 8 lamb chops,
   center cut loin or rib,
   1 to 1½-inches thick
2 tbs. olive oil, butter or
   margarine
¾ cup canned peaches,
   drained and pureed

1 medium onion, minced
½ tsp. salt
1 tbs. cider vinegar
1 to 2 tsp. molasses, or
   brown sugar
½ to 1 tsp. curry powder

Put chops in spit basket (see Spit Basket Cooking) and barbecue about 30 minutes or until done. Meanwhile, mix remaining ingredients in saucepan and cook over medium heat about 15 minutes stirring often. During last 10 minutes of barbecuing time, glaze lamb chops with sauce.

VERMOUTH VEAL CHOPS

6 loin or rib veal chops,
   about 1-inch thick
⅓ cup dry vermouth or
   white wine
1 tbs. paprika

½ cup melted butter or
   margarine
Salt and pepper to taste
½ lemon, thinly sliced

Rub each chop on both sides with vermouth or white wine. Sprinkle with paprika and let stand 30 minutes to 1 hour. Brush well with melted butter before placing on greased grill. Cook slowly over low coals, about 20 to 30 minutes, brushing with melted butter frequently. Turn once with tongs. About 5 minutes before serving top with lemon slice.

Roasts

STANDING RIB ROAST

Allow ¾ to 1 lb. per person. Have the roast sawed through the backbone to free ribs, and suet placed into the cut area. Have the ribs sawed through 2½-inches from the ends and the bone ends removed. The flap of the meat should then be tied and folded over the bone ends at 1-inch intervals with heavy twine. Season lightly with salt and pepper and secure on spit. Place drip pan under meat and use Hickory Chips and Garlic Buds or basting sauce of your choice (see recipes). Cook 17 to 25 minutes per pound, using meat thermometer to determine exact doneness. Serve with parsley, vegetable garnish and Bearnaise Sauce (see recipe).

BARBECUED RUMP ROAST

3 lbs. rump roast	1 lemon, sliced
2 cups water	12 whole cloves
2 cups vinegar	2 bay leaves
¼ cup instant minced onion	6 whole black peppercorns
	1 tsp. season salt

Combine seasoning ingredients in a bowl and mix well. Add roast and let stand 24 hours in refrigerator, turning occasionly. Spit barbecue 1½ to 2 hours, basting with remaining marinade. For grill cooking, brush marinated roast with oil and quickly brown all sides on grill. Remove to a large double-thick piece of foil and fold up sides. Add remaining marinade and seal edges well. Place roast on grill and cook 2 to 2½ hours, turning occasionally. Serve with cooking juices and vegetable garnish.

GRILLED CHUCK ROAST

1 4- to 5-lb. chuck roast, cut 2 inches thick	Salt & pepper
Meat tenderizer	Olive oil

Slit fat edges to prevent curling and tenderize chuck according to directions on tenderizer package. Sprinkle with salt and pepper and rub with oil. Place chuck on greased grill 3 inches from coals and sear on both sides, 3 to 5 minutes each. Raise grill to 6 inches above coals and cook covered with a loose sheet of heavy-duty foil. Baste with oil and turn every 15 minutes, until roast is done, about an hour — use meat thermometer to determine exact doneness. Serve roast sliced in diagonal cuts, garnished with barbecue sauce or seasoned butter (see recipes).

SPICED CHUCK ROAST

Prepare 2-inch-thick chuck roast as in Grilled Chuck Roast, marinating meat in Spanish Basting Sauce (see recipe) for 12 hours in refrigerator. Place meat on greased grill 3 inches above hot coals and sear on both sides, 3 minutes each. Raise grill 6 to 8 inches above coals and cook 1 to 1½ hours, turning every 20 minutes and basting with remaining marinade. A loose sheet of heavy-duty foil may be placed over meat to hold heat in. Use meat thermometer to determine exact doneness and serve cut into diagonal slices. (Excellent spit basket recipe and for cover cooking — see instructional chapter).

'MEAL-IN-ONE' CHUCK ROAST

3 to 5-lbs. beef chuck roast	¼ cup salad oil
3 tbs. seasoned salt	¾ cup catsup
1 large onion, sliced	½ tsp. pepper
6 medium potatoes, cut in quarters lengthwise	1 tsp. dry mustard
	1 tbs. brown sugar
6 large carrots, peeled or scraped	2 tsp, soy sauce
	2 tbs. wine vinegar

Sprinkle chuck roast with 1 tbs. seasoned salt and rub in well. Brown roast on grill over hot coals, about 15 minutes on each side. Remove roast and place on a large sheet of double-thick aluminum foil. Place sliced onion on top, potatoes and carrots around roast. Combine remaining ingredients in saucepan, cook slowly over coals stirring constantly until mixture comes to a boil; do not boil. Pour over roast and vegetables. Wrap edges of foil securely; place on grill and cook over hot coals 1½ to 2 hours. Turn with tongs several times.

EYE OF ROUND ON SPIT

Cut several shallow gashes in a 3½ lb. eye of round, and tuck in small bits of onion. Thread meat on spit and sprinkle with a dash of thyme (See Spit Cooking). Cook about 1½ to 2 hours, depending on desired doneness. Remove to heated platter, slice very thin and serve. If desired, meat may be basted during cooking with Red Wine Meat Sauce (see recipe).

ROLLED RIB OF BEEF

Use 4 to 6 lbs. rolled rib and make several small incisions in the surface and insert slivers of onion, garlic and fresh thyme. Rub surface with salad oil and sprinkle with salt. Place on spit and cook over hot coals until desired doneness. About 2½ to 3¼ hours for medium roast or 160° F. on meat thermometer. Baste frequently during cooking with marinade of your choice (see recipes).

BARBECUED LEG OF LAMB

Have butcher bone a medium-sized leg of lamb and tie securely with cord. Cut small slashes in meat and insert small bits of sliced garlic. Rub well with seasoned salt and pepper; skewer on spit. Barbecue over medium coals 2½ to 3 hours, depending on size, using a meat thermometer to determine when done. It should read 175°F. to 180°F., for medium to well done. Lamb may be marinated before cooking or basted with Lamb Basting Sauce while cooking. Excellent with Hickory Chips and Garlic Buds flavoring during cooking (see recipes).

BUTTERFLY LEG OF LAMB

1 leg of lamb, boned and butterflied	¼ tsp. each dry mint flakes, rosemary and
½ cup Lemon Butter (see recipe)	dry grated orange peel
	Pineapple slices, drained
Seasoned salt	Brown sugar
	1 tsp. cinnamon

Brush lamb with Lemon Butter and let stand at room temperature about 1 hour. Sprinkle generously with seasoned salt, mint, rosemary and orange peel. Place lamb fat side up on grill 4 to 6-inches above coals and cook 45 minutes to 1½ hours, basting often with lemon butter and turning to brown all sides. Just before meat is done (180° F. on meat thermometer), place pineapple rings on heavy duty foil and heat on grill for about 5 minutes. A few minutes before removing pineapple rings, sprinkle with brown sugar and cinnamon and serve as garnish with lamb.

JELLY GLAZED LAMB SHOULDER

3 to 4 lbs. shoulder of lamb, boned and rolled	Salt and pepper
	1½ cups currant jelly
Sliced garlic clove (if desired)	2 tsp. prepared mustard

Make several slits in roast and insert slices of garlic. Rub meat with salt and pepper. Thread lamb shoulder on spit and cook (see spit barbecuing section). Allow 25 to 30 minutes per pound or until meat thermometer reads 180° F. Place drip pan made of heavy duty foil under meat. Make a glaze by melting currant jelly and stirring in mustard. During the last 30 minutes of cooking time, baste roast with glaze.

BONE-IN LEG OF LAMB

While cooking is shortened and meat more evenly cooked with a boned leg of lamb, bone-in legs are easily cooked on a spit in a

covered unit. Prepare and season as for boned Barbecued Leg of Lamb, and insert spit carefully for good balance. Increase cooking time by 10% or use meat thermometer "done" reading of 175°F.

SMACKIN' GOOD PORK LOIN

6 lb. boneless rolled pork
  loin roast
2 tbs. olive oil
⅓ cup peanut butter

⅓ cup orange juice
Hickory chips
Clove of garlic

Tie roast with heavy cord every 1½-inches across length of meat and place on spit. Add hickory chips and garlic to coals and grill in covered unit 50 to 70 minutes, or until meat thermometer registers 185° F. Combine olive oil, peanut butter and orange juice and mix well. Baste meat with mixture and allow roast to cook 5 to 10 minutes more, or until nicely browned. Let rest 10 to 15 minutes; carve into slices at least 2-inches thick.

LEG OF PORK ON THE SPIT

1 leg of pork, boned
  (about ⅔ lb. per
  person)
⅓ cup lemon juice
⅓ cup orange juice
⅓ cup vinegar

2 cups apple cider
½ tsp. garlic salt
½ tsp. onion salt
¼ tsp. black pepper or
  cayanne

Mix all seasoning ingredients and marinate pork overnight. Drain, score leg evenly and place on spit. Brush with marinade and grill slowly over coals, allowing about 15 minutes per lb. Make a drip pan of heavy duty aluminum foil to catch pork juices for gravy. Brush often with marinade.

BUTTERFLY LEG OF PORK

3 to 5 lb. leg of pork
½ cup soy sauce
½ cup peanut oil, or
  salad oil

2 cloves garlic, minced
1 tsp. fresh ginger root,
  minced
Freshly ground pepper

Have the butcher bone leg of pork with butterfly cut and trim off the fat. Mix remaining ingredients well and pour over meat in shallow pan. Marinate overnight, turning several times. Place butterfly pork flat on grill and brown all sides. Raise grill about 6-inches from coals and barbecue slowly, turning and basting occasionally for at least 1 hour. Test for 190° F. doneness with meat thermometer.

CHINESE PORK TENDERLOIN

Cut a 2 lb. pork tenderloin in half lengthwise. Coat with a mixture of 1 tbs. soy sauce, 2 tbs. heavy molasses, 1 tbs. vinegar and ½ tsp. monosodium glutamate. Let stand at room temperature about 1 hour. Grease hot grill with pork fat. Place pork strips on grill and cook slowly, turning frequently, about 30 or 45 minutes. Serve with hot Sweet-Sour Sauce (see recipe).

SPIT-ROASTED FRESH HAM

Score and cut a 10 to 14 lb. fresh ham in half, diagonally and skewer both halves on spit. Insert meat thermometer at thickest point, and barbecue over drip pan 15 to 20 minutes per pound, or until thermometer reads 190° F. Season only with Hickory Chips and Garlic Buds on charcoal (see recipe) during cooking, serve with sauce of your choice.

PEACHY HAM

3 to 5 lbs. boneless ham, tied
½ cup peach jam

1 tbs. lemon juice
½ tsp. ground cloves

Place the ham on spit (put drip pan underneath meat), and cook about 1 hour over medium coals. Mix jam, lemon juice and cloves well and spread ham with this glaze; continue cooking about 45 minutes more, or until meat thermometer reading is 190° F. and the surface of ham is well glazed.

BARBECUED PORK BUTTS

Score and remove any casing from 2 to 3 lb. fresh pork butts. Plan ¾ lb. uncooked weight per serving. Thread on spit and barbecue over drip pan for at least 1 hour, or until meat thermometer reads 190°F. Meat may be basted with Ginger Baste For Pork, or other cooking sauce (see recipes), during last 10 minutes of cooking. Excellent when flavored with Hickory Chips and Garlic Buds on charcoal.

BARBECUED CANNED HAM

Remove excess fat and juice from ham and place on large double-thick square of heavy-duty foil. Fold up edges to seal ham completely. Place package on grill and cook until meat thermometer reads 170° F., turning occasionally. Thermometer need not be put in until after an hour for large hams. Open foil package top and baste with mixture of ½ cup pineapple juice, ¼ cup brown sugar, ¼ tsp. each, powdered clove, nutmeg and cinnamon.

Leave top open and cook 20 minutes longer, allowing charcoal fumes to penetrate ham. Serve garnished with Grilled Pineapple Slices (see recipe) and cooking juices as sauce.

Note: Whole canned hams, sealed together with gelatin, will fall apart when heated without covering. They should not be cooked on a spit or grill whole, though slices or pieces may be grilled on foil to avoid loss.

Ribs

CHEF BELL'S SPARERIBS

8 lbs. lean, meaty loin
   spareribs
½ to 1 cup olive oil
1 cup honey
1½ cups crushed
   pineapple, drained

2½ cups brown sugar
3 tsp. dry mustard
Juice of 1 lemon
Salt and pepper to taste
Hickory chips
1 garlic clove

Let ribs stand at room temperature about 1 hour before rubbing with olive oil. Add hickory chips and garlic clove to coals (see recipe). Place spareribs on grill 3 to 4-inches from coals, turning and basting often with olive oil. When meat shrinks about ¼-inch from end of bone, about 1 hour, it is done. Remove ribs to a flat pan; salt and pepper well on each side. Cut between bones to separate ribs. Mix remaining ingredients, heat and pour over ribs, coating well. Cover with foil and let stand in a warm place for 10 minutes, allowing sauce to penetrate the ribs.

QUICK GRILLED RIBS

Place about 4½ to 5 lbs. spareribs in a large kettle and cover with water. Boil the ribs about 5 minutes. This method reduces greasiness in the meat, and speeds cooking time at the grill. Drain the ribs well, and coat with a mixture of ⅔ cup soy sauce and 2 tbs. cornstarch. Grease hot grill with pork fat and lay on spareribs. Cook over medium hot fire about 20 to 30 minutes, turning each 5 minutes, or until tender. During the first 10 minutes of cooking, baste frequently with soy mixture. During last few minutes, ribs may be glazed with barbecue sauce (see recipes). Ribs are done when meat pulls away from ends of bone.

ONION SPARERIBS

Rub spareribs with salt and small amount of garlic salt, and place in a covered baking dish. Smother with sliced onions and thinly sliced lemons, cover and refrigerate overnight. Remove spareribs and thread on spit, or cook in spit basket on grill, turning often. Grill 45 minutes to 1 hour, or until done. Serve garnished with Grilled Onion Slices (see recipe).

SWEET & SOUR SPARERIBS

4 to 6 lbs. lean spareribs
1 tsp. salt
¼ cup soy sauce
¼ cup oil
⅔ cup brown sugar
⅔ cup wine vinegar

½ cup water
½ cup pineapple juice
1 tsp. grated fresh ginger
   or ¼ tsp. powdered
ginger

Rub spareribs with salt and place on grill, bone side down, or thread on spit. Grill 6 inches above coals 30 to 40 minutes, turning each 10 minutes, if on grill. Combine seasoning ingredients and brush over ribs, cooking for an additional 30 to 40 minutes, or until ribs are done (meat will pull away from end of rib bone). Continue basting and turning for even flavoring and to prevent searing. Serve with additional Sweet & Sour Sauce (see recipe) and pineapple garnish.

SPIT-BASKET RIBS

Allowing about 1 lb. per person, cut meaty spareribs into serving size pieces. Place pieces in spit basket and put a heavy duty aluminum foil drip pan under meat. Start spit motor, and barbecue ribs 45 minutes to 1 hour, or until meat is tender. Serve with sauce of your choice (see recipes) mixed with drippings. Ribs may be brushed with sauce during last few minutes of cooking or just before serving. Ribs are done when meat pulls away from ends of bone.

HAND BASKET RIBS

Cut meaty spareribs into serving-size pieces and place in a long-handled grill basket. Hold basket close to hot coals and sear ribs for about 5 minutes, turning once. Place basket on grill, and barbecue about 25 minutes longer, turning basket often. Brush with your favorite barbecue sauce (see recipe) and return to grill for about 10 to 15 minutes more, turning constantly to avoid charring.

BARBECUED SHORT RIBS

2 to 3 lbs. lean short
   ribs, 3-inches long
1½ cups tomato juice
1 tbs. brown sugar
1 tsp. salt

1 clove garlic, mashed
   (optional)
¼ tsp. cloves
⅛ tsp. thyme
1 tsp. dry mustard

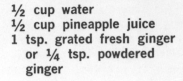

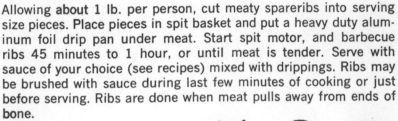

½ cup red wine vinegar
   (or dry red wine)
1 tsp. Worcestershire
   sauce

¼ cup olive or salad oil
¼ cup onions, finely
   chopped

Combine all seasoning ingredients except oil and onions, and pour over meat in a shallow pan. Refrigerate 24 to 48 hours, turning occasionally. Warm to room temperature before cooking. Add oil and onions 30 minutes before placing ribs on grill. Cook 4 inches from hot coals 30 to 40 minutes, basting and turning each 10 minutes. A loose sheet of foil may be placed over ribs to retain moisture while barbecuing. Remaining basting sauce may be boiled and spooned over cooked ribs when serving.

VARIATIONS: Substitute above marinade for any red meat marinade (see recipes) and cook in the same manner. Or, use spit or basket cooking with or without marinade. Also see Covered Cooking section. Short Ribs may also be cooked without marinades, seasoned with salt and pepper, and basted with oil during cooking.

LAMB RIBLETS

2 lbs. lamb riblets
Salt and pepper
¼ cup butter or
   margarine or olive oil
1½ tsp. salt
¼ cup cinnamon
1 cup brown sugar,
   firmly packed

½ tsp. nutmeg
½ cup orange juice
1 lemon, thinly sliced
1 cup pitted dried prunes,
   chopped
½ cup dried apricots,
   chopped

Rub lamb riblets with salt and pepper and thread on barbecue spit. Rotate over medium coals several hours or until well done. Meanwhile, melt butter in a sauce pan, add salt, cinnamon, sugar and nutmeg and stir until smooth. Add remaining ingredients, cover and cook over low heat 15 minutes, stirring occasionally. Brush mixture over lamb during last half hour of cooking. Serve riblets with remaining sauce.

ITALIAN LAMB RIBS

Have butcher cut lamb rib sections into quarters. Place in shallow pan and cover with commercial Italian-style salad dressing. Marinate for an hour or more, turning several times. Place ribs on spit or cook directly on grill, 5 inches from coals, 30 to 50 minutes, depending on thickness of ribs. Brush frequently with remaining dressing during cooking, turning every 10 minutes. A loose sheet of foil may be placed over ribs during cooking to retain heat, flavor and moisture. Ribs are done when meat is tender and pulls away from end of bone. Serve seasoned with a sprinkling of salt and pepper, parsley and tomato garnish.

MINTED LAMB RIBS

4 lbs. lamb ribs or breast
¼ cup brown sugar
1 cup orange or pineapple juice
¼ cup lemon juice

4 tbs. fresh or dried mint, chopped
½ tsp. onion powder or 1 tbs. minced onion
1 tsp. seasoning salt

Blend seasoning ingredients and pour over meat in pan. Marinate 2 to 4 hours, turning occasionally. Pour off marinade for basting sauce and cook ribs 45 minutes to an hour, either on spit or on grill, 5 to 6 inches above coals. Add ⅓ cup olive oil or salad oil to marinade and baste meat every 15 minutes, turning at the same time if grilled. Meat is done when well browned and pulls loose from ends of rib bones. Serve with fruit-type sauce (see recipes) or Grilled Pineapple Slices, garnished with additional fresh mint.

Kebobs

Variety is the secret to Kebob cooking. Unlimited combinations are available.

BURGUNDY MEAT KEBOBS

6 lbs. boneless meat (beef, lamb or pork), cut in 2-inch squares, ¾-inches thick (pork pieces should be cut smaller)
¼ cup olive oil
1 clove garlic, minced

1 bay leaf, crumbled
1 tbs. Worcestershire sauce
1½ tsp. salt
½ tsp. pepper
¾ cup onion, grated
1 tbs. parsley, chopped
Burgundy wine

Combine olive oil, garlic, bay leaf, Worcestershire sauce, salt, pepper, onion and parsley in a bowl. Add meat and enough Burgundy wine to cover. Marinate at least 4 hours or overnight; turn occasionally. Thread meat on skewers alternating with mushroom caps, small whole tomatoes, green peppers etc. Brush kebobs with marinade and place on grill 4 to 5-inches above hot coals. Grill, turning often until meat is browned on all sides, about 5 to 10 minutes, or until done. Brush several times with remaining marinade.

ORIENTAL MEAT KEBOBS

1 lb. beef tenderloin,
   cut in 1½-inch cubes
1 lb. pork tenderloin, cut
   in 1-inch cubes
1 lb. veal, cut in 1½-inch
   cubes
1 cup soy sauce

½ cup brown sugar
¼ cup peanut oil (or any
   salad oil
¼ cup sherry wine
1 tsp. monosodium
   glutamate
1 clove garlic, chopped

Combine all ingredients (except meat) and stir well. Marinate the meat cubes for 2 to 3 hours truning occasionally. Alternate marinated meat (6 to 8 cubes per kabob) on skewer, leaving about ¼ inch space between pieces. Place kebobs on greased grill about 3 to 4 inches above coals. Barbecue 10 to 12 minutes turning to brown all sides. Brush frequently with marinade.

PORK AND CHICKEN LIVER KEBOBS

1 lb. lean pork, sliced
   ¼-inch thick
1 lb. chicken livers
3 tbs. bacon drippings,
   melted butter or salad
   oil
½ cup soy sauce
⅓ cup chicken stock or
   boullion

¼ cup sherry wine or
   bourbon (or apple
   juice)
2 tbs. brown sugar
½ tsp. fresh grated
   ginger root (optional)
Dash of salt

Cut the pork into bite-size pieces. Alternate pork with chicken livers on skewers (don't pack meat too closely). Mix remaining ingredients and blend well. Marinate the kebobs in this mixture 1 to 2 hours, turning often. Barbecue about 4 to 5-inches from coals turning and basting frequently with marinade. Cook until well browned and pork is well done, about 15 to 25 minutes.

PORK CHUNKS TERIYAKI

Using pork butt or shoulder, cut chunks about ¼ to ½-inches thick and marinate in Teriyaki Marinade (see recipe), 1 to 2 hours at room temperature, turning several times. Drain and place in spit basket or grill on skewers turning often and brushing with marinade. Cook 20 to 30 minutes, or until done.

SPICED BURGER KEBOBS

2 lbs. ground beef, or
   lamb
1 small bunch green
   onions, chopped

⅛ tsp. each of the
   following: cinnamon,
   cloves, cumin, red
   pepper, coriander and

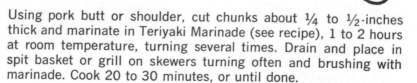

46

1 tsp. salt   paprika

Combine all ingredients and let mixture stand for 1 hour at room temperature. Shape into meat balls (large or small depending if to be used as appetizer or main course). Thread carefully on skewers and cook on grill, turning until evenly browned on all sides.

HAWAIIAN LAMB KABOBS

1 lb. lamb shoulder, cut in 1½-inch cubes
1 1-lb. 4½-oz. can pineapple chunks, (save syrup)
Cherry tomatoes
Fresh mushrooms, washed
1 green pepper, cubed
¼ cup vinegar
¼ cup honey

3 tbs. butter, melted, or peanut oil
1 clove garlic, minced
1 tsp. Worcestershire sauce
1 tsp. salt
¼ tsp.pepper
¼ tsp. ginger (or 1 tsp. fresh grated ginger root)

Alternate lamb cubes with pineapple, tomatoes, mushrooms and peppers on skewers. Combine remaining ingredients with drained pineapple syrup and mix well. Brush kebobs with mixture and cook over medium coals 15 to 20 minutes, basting and turning occasionally.

HAM KABOBS

Thread 1 inch cubes of precooked ham and chunks of pineapple on skewers. If desired, stud the pineapple with a few whole cloves. Cook on lightly greased grill, turning often, until pineapple is lightly browned and meat thoroughly heated. May be basted with a mixture of pineapple juice and brown sugar.

VARIATIONS: Along with ham and pineapple pieces, alternate any combination of, cherry tomatoes, pepper slices, pearl onions, frozen-type potato fritters, cooked sweet potato pieces or virtually any firm, fresh fruit.

HEART EN BROCHETTE

2 lbs. heart, beef or lamb
¾ cup wine vinegar
2 fresh chili peppers or
¼ tsp. cayenne

2 cloves garlic, minced
1 tsp. salt
½ cup water
¼ cup olive oil

Wash heart and trim off tubes and membranes. Cut into 1-inch cubes and combine with all ingredients except oil. Marinate overnight refrigerated, turning a few times. Place heart loosely on skewers and brush with oil. Barbecue 3 inches from coals 10 to

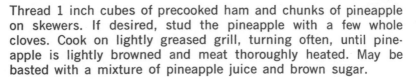

12 minutes, basting with oil and turning often. Serve with Barbecue Sauce and Vegetable Kebobs (see recipes).

LIVER & BACON EN BROCHETTE

2 lbs. liver, 1-inch thick
¼ tsp. sage
1 tsp. monosodium
  glutamate
½ cup peanut or olive oil

¼ tsp. pepper
¼ tsp. onion salt or
  garlic salt
6 to 8 strips of bacon

Soak liver in mild salt-water solution (1 tsp. salt to 2 cups of water) for 20 to 30 minutes; drain and dry on paper towel. Mix sage, monosodium glutamate, oil, onion salt and pepper in shallow pan. Marinate liver 2 to 3 hours in refrigerator, turning several times. To make kebobs, start with strip of bacon and weave through and over liver chuck and through bacon, then liver and etc. Brush well with marinade and place kebobs on grill over medium coals for 12 to 16 minutes, turning until all sides are done. Do not overcook, the liver should be slightly pink on the inside.

TURKISH LIVER KEBOBS

1 lb. beef or lamb liver
Juice of 1 lemon
¼ cup olive oil

4 bay leaves
½ tsp. cardamom, ground
Salt and pepper

Cut the liver into cubes (about 1½-inches). Mix remaining ingredients and marinate liver cubes in shallow pan for 1 hour. Drain and thread on skewers, alternate with bay leaf about every two liver cubes. Cook over hot coals, about 5 to 8 minutes, or until liver is browned on all sides. Baste frequently with remaining marinade.

SWEETBREAD KEBOBS

1½ lbs. (2 pairs) veal or
  lamb sweetbreads
2 qts. water
2 tbs. vinegar
2 tbs. salt

¼ lb. butter, melted
½ cup cracker or bread
  crumbs
12 fresh mushrooms,
  washed

Bring water, vinegar and salt solution to a boil and simmer sweetbreads 15 to 20 minutes. Drain and drop into ice water to cool. Trim off membranes and cut sweetbreads into 1½-inch pieces. Dip into melted butter and dust with crumbs. Alternate pieces on skewers with mushrooms and grill 3 inches above coals, turning every few minutes and brushing with butter. Sweetbreads are done when evenly browned. A little sherry may be sprinkled over kebobs during final minutes of cooking for added flavor. Serve with seasoned butter and lemon slice garnish.

Ground Meat & Specialties

ROMANO VEAL PATTIES

2 lbs. veal, chopped or
    ground (also beef or
    lamb)
½ tsp. anchovy paste
1 clove garlic, mashed

Olive oil
¼ tsp. pepper
¼ tsp. oregano (or
    Italian seasoning)

Mix anchovy paste and ground veal blending in about 1 tsp. of olive oil. Add remaining ingredients, except olive oil, and mix thoroughly. Shape into 6 patties about ¾-inch thick, brush with oil and place on grill. Barbecue 5 to 8 minutes on each side over medium hot coals; brush frequently with olive oil.

MEAT LOAF IN FOIL

2 lbs. ground beef
¼ lb. ground pork
1 cup bread crumbs
½ cup tomato juice
1 egg, slightly beaten
¼ cup onion, minced

2 tbs. parsley, minced
¼ tsp. thyme
¼ tsp. tabasco sauce
2 tsp. salt
¼ tsp. pepper

Mix the meat with remaining ingredients and shape into loaf. Place on double-thickness of heavy aluminum foil that has been coated on inside with salad oil. Wrap edges securely and place on grill over medium coals, for about 1-1½ hours. Using tongs, turn meat loaf several times. Slice and serve with barbecue sauce or your choice of relish (see recipes).

GRILLED HASH IN FOIL

Open a large can of corned beef or roast beef hash, and carefully remove contents in one piece. Cut hash into thick slices, and place each slice in individual foil packages that you have buttered on the inside. Seal packages, and place on grill. Cook about 5 to 7 minutes each side, turning once or twice. Garnish with parsley and serve immediately.

GRILLED SAUSAGES

All sausages, breakfast type pork links, Polish sausage, knackwurst, bratwurst, etc., become elegant fare when charcoal

grilled. So simply place on grill (parallel to grids to prevent rolling) and cook 3 inches above coals for small varieties, 6 inches above for large sausages. Always turn with tongs to prevent punctures and loss of juices. Sausages are done when evenly browned, or when bubbling with juices under the skins.

GRILLED HEART

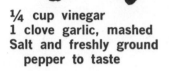

1 beef heart, cut into
  ½-inch slices
¾ cup olive oil, or salad
  oil
¾ cup dry red dinner
  wine

¼ cup vinegar
1 clove garlic, mashed
Salt and freshly ground
  pepper to taste

Blend all ingredients together and marinate beef heart for 3 to 4 hours, or overnight, turning several times. Grill about 3 to 4-inches from coals, 3 to 5 minutes on each side brushing frequently with marinade. Heart is done when center is soft-pink color when edge is cut. Serve with Grilled Onion Slices as relish (see recipe).

GRILLED LIVER

Use veal, beef, lamb or pork liver that is sliced at least 1-inch thick. Brush with salad oil, bacon drippings or melted, seasoned butters (see recipes). Place liver on grill 3 to 4-inches from coals; grill until crisp and brown on the outside and about medium rare in the middle(make a slit with sharp knife to test degree of doneness. Turn with tongs once or twice.

GRILLED KIDNEYS

Cut a pair of kidneys (per serving) in half and soak 2 hours in enough cold water to cover, plus 2 tbs. vinegar and 1 tsp. salt. Drain and trim off membranes and cord. Dry on paper towel and brush with olive oil or salad oil. Season with salt and pepper or seasoned salt. Place kidneys on greased grill, 5 inches above coals, and cook 8 to 10 minutes, turning often and brushing with additional oil. Kidneys are done when inside is pale pink color when edge is cut. Serve with seasoned butter or table sauce (see recipes).

CORNED BEEF OR TONGUE ON THE SPIT

Steam or boil a corned beef or tongue until tender. Drain well and cool to allow easy handling. Rub meat with oil, 1 tsp. chili powder and ½ tsp. onion salt. Thread on spit and roast until nicely browned, brushing occasionally with oil. Slice and serve hot with horseradish or hot mustard.

GRILLED VEAL CUTLET

2 lbs. veal cutlet, 1-inch
   thick
Juice of 2 lemons
1 tbs. chives or shallots,
   minced

2 tbs. parsley, minced
½ clove garlic, mashed
⅓ cup melted butter, or
   salad oil
Salt and pepper

Place veal cutlet in shallow pan. Mix remaining ingredients well and pour over meat. Marinate at least 2 hours. Turn meat frequently. Place cutlet on grill 4 to 5-inches above coals and cook slowly 25 minutes, turning once or twice. Baste frequently with remaining marinade. Serve with Shallot Butter Sauce (see recipe).

GRILLED BEEF STEW

To a large can of beef stew, add a dash of oregano and about ½ tsp. monosodium glutamate, and a few drops of Tabasco for extra zest. Spoon the stew onto double thicknesses of heavy duty foil, and seal into individual packages. Place packages on the grill and cook until thoroughly heated, about 20 minutes. Turn occasionally. The stew may be eaten directly from the foil. Serve with a hot bread such as garlic bread. For charcoal flavor, open foil packet 5 minutes before removing from grill.

BARBECUED BACON

Extra thick slices of bacon or Canadian bacon may be cooked directly on the grill, though excessive fat drippings may cause flareup. The most reliable way to barbecue bacon is to shape a "frying pan" out of a double thickness of heavy-duty foil and cook bacon in the "pan" placed on the grill over hot coals. The charcoal flavor is still imparted into the bacon's rich flavor, especially if done in a covered unit or with another piece of foil loosely placed over the "pan" to capture fumes above the meat.

SPIT ROASTED CANADIAN BACON

1½ lb. Canadian bacon,
   whole
¼ cup maple syrup

¼ cup orange juice
⅛ tsp. ground cloves

On surface of bacon, make diagonal cuts, ⅛-inch deep at ¾-inch intervals repeating at an angle to make squares. Combine other ingredients to make the basting sauce. Secure Canadian bacon on spit, and place about 4-inches above hot coals. Cook 30 to 45 minutes basting with sauce every 5 minutes. Recipe may also be cooked on grill, basting and turning often. Hickory Chips (see recipe) may be added to coals.

POULTRY

The secret in barbecuing turkey is in the proper seasoning and preparation prior to cooking. Then, with the use of modern spit barbecue cooking, your turkey will turn out to be the best ever. See instructions for seasoning with Hickory Chips & Garlic Buds (recipe). Note proper placement of spit and how wings and legs are secured with cord.

Turkey

SPIT-BARBECUED TURKEY

SELECTION: Choose well-shaped birds (the broad-breasted "butter ball" variety are best) of from 10 to 18 lbs. Frozen turkeys should be thawed according to wrapper directions and warmed to room temperature before preparation. Birds larger than 18 lbs. should be cooked in halves (see recipe) either on grill or spit.

PREPARATION: Wash turkey well inside and out with cold water. Pat dry with paper towel and rub well with olive oil, inside and out, followed by a liberal sprinkling of salt and pepper—inside and out. Tie the hind legs together in a crossed position, pulling them down so that they can be secured to the tail. Pull the loose neck skin back as far as possible onto the back and secure with skewers. Insert the spit rod (with back forks in position) through the turkey from the back, passing in between the tied legs and tail and through the pelvic bone. Press or hammer the spit rod through the center of the breast bone section so that it comes out in the exact center of the front (neck) section. If properly placed, the bird will "ride" on its wishbone along the spit. Center turkey on spit rod and insert rear forks solidly into meat and bone just behind the tail. Insert front forks into breast sections as far as possible and tighten both set skrews with pliers. Tie wings and legs tightly to body with additional cords (as pictured) as well as secure leg ends and tail to rod with several ties. Lift turkey by spit ends and rotate for balance. Make and corrections. Sprinkle turkey with paprika and place in cooking position over medium coals, using a drip pan (see instructional chapter).

OPEN COOKING: An average turkey will take from 4 to 5 lbs. of charcoal briquets, though not all at once. Start with a double or triple row of fully lighted briquets piled at the back of the fire pan (see instructional chapter) and add additional briquets as required. Small turkeys will cook in 2 hours, large birds require up to 5 hours. Insert meat thermometer into thickest section of breast, not touching bone, to determine when done. Baste turkey with oil and season coals with Hickory Chips & Garlic Buds (see recipe). Watch skin to see that it does not blister. Lower fire pan or spread out coals if blistering occurs. Turkey is done when thermometer reaches 190°F. Remove turkey from unit and place in a warm spot for 15 to 20 minutes to "set up" before removing spit and carving. Drip pan juices may be saved for gravy making. Serve with festive fruit or parsley garnish and cranberry sauce.

COVERED COOKING: Prepare turkey the same as for open cooking and spit barbecue at a covered temperature of 320°F. Cooking time will be reduced by 20% from open cooking time—use meat thermometer reading of 190°F. to determine when done. Use Hickory Chips & Garlic Buds (see recipe).

STUFFING: Turkeys cook more evenly on a spit if unstuffed as the heat penetrates into the meat from inside and out. Stuffed turkeys may be spit-barbecued, though special attention must be taken to keep stuffing from coming out during hours of turning. If pre-stuffed, or if stuffing turkey yourself, be sure that the cavity is not more than ⅔rds full. The stuffing can expand and burst the bird on the spit if filled too full. Use a bread stuffing, not rice or one which will be difficult to keep inside bird. Before closing cavity, form a "boot" out of double-thick heavy duty foil and fit it in between the stuffing and the inside edges of the cavity to close the opening completely. Next, secure skin over opening with cord and tie legs and tail in position (see photo). Tie wings to breast and insert and balance spit per above directions. Cooking time will increase 20% or so over unstuffed turkey recipe. Use meat thermometer reading of 190°F to determine when done.

GRILL-ROASTED HALF TURKEY

Medium to small turkey halves may be roasted directly on an open grill and are especially suited to covered unit cooking. Have butcher split turkey into full-side halves. Rinse well, dry and coat with oil, salt, pepper and paprika. (Turkey may be marinated if desired—see recipes.) Place on oiled grill 6 to 8 inches over medium to low coals. Brown on both sides, about 15 minutes each, basting frequently. Cover with a loose sheet of heavy-duty foil to hold in heat and continue cooking 1 to 1½ hours, turning and basting every 15 minutes. Turkey is done when meat thermometer reaches 190°F. Note: for covered or barrel unit, sear with lid open (per above) and close lid after second side is browned. Turn and baste every 20 minutes, reducing total cooking time by 20%.

BARBECUED TURKEY WINGS

Use 6 to 8 turkey wings cut apart at joints to make flat pieces. Follow the same methods and sauces as for turkey quarters, however, cooking time need not be as long. Turkey is done when meat is fork tender and no red juice appears when skin is pricked. Cooking time will be 35 to 60 minutes, depending on wing size, over medium coals. Brush with barbecue sauce during final 10 minutes of cooking (see recipes) if desired.

FOIL ROAST TURKEY QUARTERS

Wash and dry turkey quarters. Marinate (see recipes) for approximately 2 hours. Sprinkle with seasoning salt. Place marinated turkey quarters on large sheet of heavy-duty aluminum foil. Pad sharp bony ridges with additional foil to prevent break-through of outside foil. Fold foil over the top of the pieces and seal edges tightly. Place packets with bony cavity down on the grill 4 inches from coals for about 45 minutes. Turn with tongs and cook meaty side down, 45 minutes more. Turn again; insert thermometer through foil top and barbecue until it reads 180°F. Remove turkey from grill, take off foil, saving juices. Return turkey to grill and brush frequently with marinade to which turkey juices have been added. Continue barbecuing until skin is browned on both sides, about 20 minutes longer.

GRILLED TURKEY QUARTERS

Follow Spit-Roasted Turkey Quarters recipe for preparation and seasoning. Place on oiled grill, 6 to 8 inches from coals and cook 40 to 60 minutes, depending on size. Baste and turn quarters every 10 minutes. Turkey is done when meat thermometer reaches 190°F. and joints feel loose when twisted. Note: A loose sheet of foil may be placed over the turkey, shiny side down, to speed cooking and hold in moisture.

SPIT-ROASTED TURKEY ROLL

Thaw turkey roll according to wrapper directions if frozen and rinse in cold water. Dry with paper towel and rub with olive oil, salad oil or melted butter. Sprinkle with salt, pepper, and paprika. Insert spit rod through center, tighten forks and check for balance. Cook over medium to low coals, using a drip pan, basting with oil every 20 minutes. A 3 to 5 lb. turkey roll will cook in 2 to 2½ hours, a 7 to 9 lb. roll in 2½ to 3 hours. Check for doneness with meat thermometer reading of 190°F. Remove from spit and cut away cord ties. Slice in thin cross-cuts and serve with natural juices from drip pan, tomato or fruit garnish. For added flavor, any of the poultry marinades and basting sauces may be used for turkey (see recipes).

SPIT ROASTED TURKEY QUARTERS

1 6- to 8-lb. turkey, quartered
1 6-oz. can orange juice concentrate, thawed and undiluted
2 lbs. candied ginger, chopped
2 lbs. soy sauce
Dash of Tabasco sauce
1 tsp. salt
1 clove of garlic, crushed

Rinse turkey parts, dry on paper towel. Place parts in shallow pan. Mix the other ingredients and pour over turkey, marinate in the refrigerator 3 hours or overnight, turning several times. Remove from marinade and place parts on spit rod, securing with forks and tying with cord if center parts are loose. Check for balance and place over medium coals. Baste frequently and cook 1½ to 2 hours, or until meat thermometer reads 190°F. Heat remaining marinade with drip pan juices and serve with turkey as sauce.

Chicken &
Cornish Hens

SPIT BARBECUED WHOLE CHICKENS

Select 2 to 3½ lb. chickens, ½ chicken per serving. Wash thoroughly and dry with paper towel. Sprinkle inside cavity with salt and pepper and place on spit. Run spit rod through chicken parallel to the backbone, from a point inside from the neck to just inside the tail and legs. Legs and wings should be tied if loose. Place second (or each additional chicken) "breast opposite" in up and down position for balance. Press together and insert spit forks. Test for good balance and make any adjustment. Coat outsides with olive oil and sprinkle well with salt, pepper and paprika. Place spit 4 inches from medium coals and position drip pan. Baste with oil every 10 minutes on open unit (covered units need no basting) and cook 40 to 60 minutes, depending on size of chickens. They are done when meat is tender and pulls easily away from the bone and joints feel loose when legs are twisted. Remove chickens from spit and snip loose twine. Cut in halves with kitchen shears through back and breastbone and serve with barbecue sauce which has been mixed with drip pan juices.

SPIT-BASKET CHICKEN

Chicken parts, quarters and halves are excellent for spit-basket cooking. Prepare according to grill recipe for seasoning and marinating, but place parts in an oiled spit basket. Place in position over coals with motor off. Sear chicken 5 minutes on each side, turning basket over. Start motor and cook 45 to 60 minutes on open unit, 40 to 50 minutes on barrel or covered units at 325°F.

BARBECUED CHICKEN HALVES & QUARTERS

Rinse chicken pieces well and dry on paper towel. Parts may be marinated in any of several poultry marinades (see recipes) if desired, or seasoned only with olive oil, salt, pepper and paprika. Place parts skin-side down on a greased grill, over medium coals and sear for 3 minutes. Turn and sear the other side 3 minutes and raise grill to 5 inches or more. Baste with remaining marinade or oil and cook 35 to 45 minutes, turning and basting every 5 minutes. Chicken is done when meat pulls easily away from bone and joints feel loose when legs are twisted.

SKEWERED CHICKEN WINGS

Place chicken wings on kebob skewers so that they will lie flat on the grill. Follow Grilled Chicken Parts recipe, reducing searing and cooking time by a few minutes to avoid overcooking. Excellent served as hors d'oeuvre or snacks.

CHICKEN & BARBECUE SAUCE

Prepare chicken parts or quarters according to Grilled Chicken Parts recipe, increasing cooking time 5 to 10 minutes for quarters. During the final 10 minutes of cooking, baste chicken with Western Barbecue Sauce (see recipe), turning so that each side is glazed with sauce, but not burned.

GRILLED CHICKEN PARTS

Rinse parts well and dry on paper towel. Brush with oil and sprinkle with salt and pepper. For color, sprinkle liberally with paprika. Place parts on an oiled grill and sear 5 minutes on each side, 3 to 4 inches from coals. Raise grill to 6 inches and continue cooking 25 to 30 minutes, basting and turning every 5 minutes. Smaller parts, such as wings and legs, will cook faster than the larger ones, and may be placed at the outside edge of the grill to avoid overcooking. Chicken is done when meat is tender and pulls easily away from bone.

CHICKEN TERIYAKI

Prepare chicken parts or quarters according to Grilled Chicken Parts recipe, omitting seasoning. Instead, marinate chicken in Teriyaki Marinade (see recipe) for 20 minutes before grilling and use marinade as basting sauce.

HERBED CHICKEN

Marinate chicken parts, quarters or halves in Herbed Chicken Marinade, (see recipe) and barbecue according to grill or spit cooked chicken recipes, using marinade as basting sauce.

CHICKEN LIVER KEBOBS

Cut 1½ lbs. chicken livers in half and season with salt and pepper. Alternate on skewers with bite-sized pieces of tomato, green pepper and onion. Brush with oil and grill 5 inches over medium coals 10 to 15 minutes, or until liver is firm and cooked through, turning and basting with oil frequently. Serve immediately as entree or hors d'oeuvre.

VARIATIONS: Alternate chicken liver pieces with squares of bacon, fresh mushrooms or fruit, such as pineapple or fresh peach. Serve topped with Sweet & Sour Sauce (see recipe).

SPIT ROASTED GAME HENS

(Rock Cornish Hens)
Follow recipe for Spit Barbecued Whole Chickens, only place a half an apple and half an onion in cavity. Season with salt and pepper and cook over medium coals 50 minutes to 1 hour, basting with melted butter, Hot Sauce or Herb Butter (see recipes) every 10 minutes. Hens are done when leg joints feel loose when twisted.

SEAFOODS

Fish

GRILLED FISH STEAKS
(For Halibut, Salmon, Haddock, Swordfish etc.)

Select fresh or frozen fish steaks, cut at least 1-inch thick. Thaw frozen steaks and marinate in Seafood Marinade (see recipe) for about ½ hr. before cooking, if desired. Brush fish steaks with melted butter or oil and place on grill 4-inches over medium coals. Turn only once after about 6 minutes and cook another 6 minutes or until meat flakes with a fork. If unmarinated, season to taste with salt and pepper and serve sprinkled with lemon juice and melted butter. Garnish with paprika and lemon slices.

GRILLED SMALL WHOLE FISH

Allowing 2 small fish per person, clean and if desired, remove heads. Wash well and pat dry with paper towels. Make a thin paste of equal parts of oil and flour, and season with salt and pepper. Coat each fish with paste, and place on grill over medium-hot coals. Barbecue 6 to 8 minutes, turning once, or until fish is easily flaked with a fork.

VARIATION: For easier turning of very small or delicate fish, fold a piece of clean chicken wire in half and lay fish inside. Place package flat on grill and turn all at once. Serve with lemon slice and parsley garnish.

TANGY FISH BARBECUE

3 lbs. fish sticks or whole fish	Juice of 1 lemon
	1 tsp. onion or garlic salt
1 6-oz. can frozen grapefruit juice concentrate, thawed	¼ tsp. dry mustard
	¼ tsp. Tabasco sauce
	¼ tsp. thyme

Combine grapefruit and lemon juices and onion salt, mustard, Tabasco and thyme. Place fish on grill 3-inches over hot coals and grill, basting often with juice mixture until fish is done and flakes easily with fork. Spoon remaining juice mixture over fish when serving.

FOIL-WRAPPED WHOLE FISH

6 small fish, whole
1/4 lb. melted butter

Salt and pepper
Juice of 3 lemons

Brushed cleaned fish inside and out with butter and sprinkle with salt and pepper. Wrap each in aluminum foil, dull side out, and secure edges tightly. Place on grill and cook from 25 to 30 minutes, depending on size, or until fish flakes with a fork. Open foil to let in barbecue smoke during final 5 minutes. Remove fish from foil and sprinkle with lemon juice. Serve garnished with parsley and with additional butter.

SPIT-BARBECUED LARGE FISH

Large, whole round shaped fish may be barbecued in a variety of ways. Dry-meat varieties, will require basting with seasoned butter or an oil-base sauce, or stuffed with partially cooked bacon or saugage. Oily-meat varieties are best basted with juice or wine basting sauces (see recipes) and may be stuffed 2/3 full with your favorite bread-type stuffing, if desired. Stuffed fish should be tied well or sewn closed with cord to hold in stuffing. Bacon slices may be wrapped around outside for added flavor to both varieties.

Clean fish well and remove head. Season inside and out with salt and pepper, and melted butter or salad oil for dry meat varieties. If fish is to be marinated, allow at least 1/2 hour in marinade before cooking. Since fish becomes very delicate and easily broken when cooked, it is well to wrap the fish in a clean piece of chicken wire, securing it closed tightly around the length of the fish. Insert spit and secure forks through wire into fish. A 6 lb. fish will cook in approximately 1 hour, turned 6 inches above medium coals. Fish is done when meat flakes easily. Unwrap wire and remove fish with care. Serve in whole cross-section pieces or lift off meaty sections from sides for boneless portions. Garnish with lemon wedges, parsley and paprika.

SALMON & MUSHROOM BAKE

2 lbs. salmon steaks or
  fillets
1 tsp. salt
Pepper to taste

1/4 cup melted butter
1/4 cup sliced mushrooms,
2 tbs. lemon juice
2 tsp. grated onion

Combine all seasoning ingredients. Place pieces of salmon in separate packages made of double sheets of heavy-duty aluminum foil, and just before sealing, spoon sauce onto each fish. Place on grill and bake 35 minutes, or until fish flakes easily with fork.

59

SALMON KEBOBS

2 lbs. salmon steaks or fillets, in 1-inch cubes	2 tsp. salt
1 cup catsup	1/8 tsp. Tabasco
1/4 cup brown sugar	1/4 tsp. Worcestershire
1/4 cup vinegar	6 tbs. oil

Thread salmon cubes on skewers. Combine remaining ingredients. Marinate salmon in sauce for 2 hours, turning occasionally. Place skewered fish on grill and cook, turning once, about 20 minutes, or until fish flakes easily with fork. Baste occasionally during cooking with remaining marinade.

FRESH GRILLED TROUT

Clean trout, slit up belly and flatten fish out. Place on grill over low coals flesh side down until it has browned a bit. Turn fish over and season with salt and pepper; brush melted butter over the upper side to keep the meat from drying out. Cook slowly over the coals until the skin side of trout is brittle crisp, 10 to 15 minutes. Serve immediately, topped with lemon slices and Lemon Butter (see recipe). Note: For easier turning, lay trout inside a flat, folded piece of clean chicken wire, and grill as usual, turning all at once within wire.

RAINBOW TROUT & BACON

6 Rainbow trout, cleaned fresh or frozen	2 tbs. parsley, minced
2 tbs. condensed milk	1/2 tsp. nutmeg or allspice
1/2 tsp. garlic salt	12 slices bacon

Blend milk, garlic salt, parsley and nutmeg; coat trout inside and out with mixture. Wrap bacon around trout and secure with pick. Place on greased grill and cook 15 to 20 minutes, turning so that bacon cooks evenly to a crisp. Serve with additional parsley and lemon wedges.

Shellfish

GRILLED LOBSTER

Cut or saw par-boiled lobsters in half (see Lobster & Crab Steamer recipe) and rinse out insides in cold water. Dry with paper towel and brush centers and tail meat with melted butter. Rub grill with butter and place lobster halves on, cut side down. Sear 3 minutes or so, only until tail meat is lightly golden in spots. Turn lobsters

and raise grill to 5 inches. Baste well with melted butter or Lemon Butter (see recipe) and cover lightly with a sheet of heavy duty foil to hold in heat. Cook about 10 minutes longer basting often with butter. Serve in the shells with additional melted butter, Drawn Butter or seasoned butter, garnished with lemon wedges and parsley.

GRILLED LOBSTER TAILS

Large lobster tails should be cut in half from top to bottom. Small tails need only the bottom covering removed to expose the tail meat. Grill according to Grilled Lobster recipe (though cooking time may be reduced for small tail portions.)

BARBECUED CLAWS & LEGS

Lobster or crab claws and Alaska crab legs are easily cooked over charcoal. Wash outsides well and leave whole. Place on grill 3-inches above coals and cook 5 to 10 minutes on each side, turning with tongs. Just before serving, lift from grill with tongs and place on solid surface. Crack tops with a hammer and return to grill. Pour melted butter or Lemon Butter (see recipe) into cracked top. Cook a minute or two longer and serve with lemon wedges and parsley garnish.

BARBECUED STUFFED CRAB

1 lb. crab meat
⅓ cup butter or
   margarine, melted
2 tbs. lemon juice
¼ tsp. salt

Dash of cayenne pepper
¼ cup chopped parsley
6 crab shells, washed
   and greased

Pick over crab meat, removing any shell or cartilage. Combine butter, lemon juice, salt, cayenne and crab meat. Place in prepared shells, and wrap each crab individually in double thicknesses of heavy duty foil. Bury in hot coals and barbecue 7 to 10 minutes or place on grill and broil 12 to 16 minutes or until brown. Garnish with chopped parsley and serve in shells.

BARBECUE LOBSTER & CRAB STEAMER

Large portable barbecue units make excellent steamers for lobster and crab. Kettles may be placed directly on the grill over hot coals, or supported (for heavy kettles) with iron rods across the fire bowl rim. Fill kettle 2/3rds full with hot water, or bring cold water to a boil. Add a little salt (about 1 tsp. per quart) and drop in live lobsters, head-first. Cover and cook 20 minutes after water boils again. Remove lobsters and split in halves. Clean with running water and serve "just boiled" with Lemon Butter, or grill according to recipes.

SHELLFISH KEBOBS

Lobster, shrimp, scallops, oysters and other shellfish may be mixed or skewered alike for kebobs. Fresh or thawed frozen seafood may be used, cutting large pieces of parboiled lobster tail into bite-size pieces. Shrimp may be peeled (leaving the last section and tail on) or cooked unpeeled. Alternate with such items as pineapple, onion, pepper, stuffed olives, cherry tomatoes, lemon wedges and bacon or ham slice squares. Baste with Lemon or Herb Butter, or marinate Seafood Marinade (see recipes). Grill 5 inches from coals for 10 to 15 minutes, basting and turning often for even cooking.

SOUTH SEA SCALLOPS

1 lb. fresh scallops or
    frozen scallops, thawed
6 pineapple slices
1 tsp. salt

Dash white pepper
¼ cup brown sugar,
    firmly packed
Butter or margarine

Wash scallops, and if very large, cut in halves. Place pineapple slices on individual double thick heavy-duty aluminum foil. Put scallops in center of each pineapple slice, and sprinkle with salt, pepper and brown sugar. Dot with butter, and seal foil packages. Place on grill and barbecue about 20 minutes, or until scallop flakes with fork.

SCALLOP KEBOBS

1½ lbs. whole scallops
½ lb. medium size fresh
    mushrooms, washed

6 slices bacon cut in
    squares
French dressing

Alternate scallops, mushrooms and bacon squares on skewers. Brush with highly seasoned French dressing and grill over hot charcoal on grill about 10 minutes, basting often with dressing.

SCALLOPS IN SHELLS

2 lbs. fresh or frozen
  scallops
Juice of 1 lemon
¼ lb. butter, melted
¼ cup catsup
Salt and pepper

1½ cups cracker or
    bread crumbs
¼ cup chopped parsley
1 green onion, minced
6 scallop baking shells

Brush inside of shells (or shell-shaped foil cups) with butter and place in as many rinsed scallops as will fit loosely. Sprinkle with lemon juice. Blend remaining ingredients and spoon over scallops. Wrap each shell in a double-thickness of foil and place on grill, shell-side down. Cook 20 to 30 minutes, opening package at top during final 5 minutes. Pour in additional melted butter if required. Scallops are done when firm and sauce is steaming hot.

SHRIMP KEBOBS

1½ lb. shrimp, fresh or
    thawed frozen
4 slices bacon, cut in
    squares
1 4-oz. can button
    mushrooms, drained

½ tsp. salt
Dash of pepper
3 tbs. butter or
    margarine, melted
1 tbs. lemon juice

Combine butter, lemon juice and salt and pepper. Peel, devein and wash shrimp and pat dry with paper towels. Alternate shrimp, bacon squares and mushrooms on skewers and brush with seasoned butter. Place on grill over hot coals and broil about 5 minutes; turn and brush with more butter and broil 3 to 5 minutes longer. Serve with lemon wedges.

JUMBO SHRIMP KEBOBS

Shell very large shrimp or prawns, leaving last section and tail on. Rinse well and devein if desired. Shrimps may be marinated in any of the seafood cooking sauces (see recipes) for an hour. Thread on skewers in "U" shape, with a large stuffed olive or onion in the center. The skewer should pass through each shrimp twice, at large end and tail. Brush with additional marinade, melted butter or oil and barbecue over medium coals 10 to 15 minutes. turn every few minutes and baste; shrimp are done when bright pink and meat is white and firm in center. Serve garnished with parsley, lemon wedges. Unmarinated shrimp may be served with a spiced catsup or barbecue sauce dip.

SHRIMP ORIENTAL

3 lb. large shrimp,
    shelled and cleaned
½ cup melted butter or
    margarine

¼ cup lemon juice
3 tbs. chopped parsley
½ cup soy sauce

Marinate shrimp in soy sauce for 10 minutes, turning frequently. Thread on skewers and place on grill about 7 inches from coals. Mix lemon juice and butter, and baste shrimp with this mixture often during cooking. Grill shrimp 9 minutes, turn and broil other side for about 3 minutes. Remove from grill to hot platter, and pour over remaining lemon butter. Sprinkle with fresh chopped parsley.

VARIATION: This recipe can also be used for other shellfish such as prawns, crayfish, lobster tails, or small fish such as sardines, smelts, etc.

OLD FASHIONED CLAM BAKE

4 dozen fresh clams, in shells	6 lemons, cut in wedges
1 lb. melted butter	Salt & pepper

Clean clam shells under cold water with vegetable brush. Adjust grill to 3 inches above hot coals. Lay clams on grill, one shell directly down to hold juice. When top shell opens, calms are ready to be sprinkled quickly with butter, juice, salt and pepper. Serve immediately right in shells. Hot sauce or other seasonings may also be added.

CLAMS OR OYSTERS "LA PLANCHA"

1 doz. large fresh clams or oysters	¼ tsp. garlic salt
½ cup catsup	Dash Tabasco sauce
¼ cup olive oil, or salad oil	2 tsp. onion, minced fine
Juice of 2 lemons	½ cup bread crumbs
	1 tsp. oregano

Open shells and remove inedible parts, and loosen meat with knife, rinse with water. Set shells, each containing its own meat, on grill 4-inches from coals and quickly spoon in a mixture of seasoning ingredients, topped with a pinch of bread crumbs. As soon as sauce boils slightly in the center, the clams or oysters are done. Serve hot and eat with wooden picks.

OYSTERS EN BROCHETTE

1 pint oysters, drained	Pearl onions
6 slices bacon	Salt and pepper to taste
Cherry tomatoes	

Cut the bacon in 2-inch squares. Alternate bacon, oysters, tomato and pearl onions on skewers. Sprinkle with salt and pepper, and grill over hot coals about 25 minutes, turning often, or until bacon is crisp.

BACON-WRAPPED OYSTERS

Wrap drained oysters in slices of bacon; fasten with picks. Grill over hot coals, about 5 minutes, turning with tongs until bacon is crisp all over. Serve as hors d' oeurve or entree with lemon wedges.

The Colorful Foods Of Barbecue

The succulent flavors of charcoal cooking are rivaled only by the eye-catching colors of the barbecued foods themselves. Chef Ed Bell's patio party menu couples vivid garnish with a variety of taste selections. Favorites for all make up his informal buffet of easy-to-cook dishes, prepared on two units, a covered barrel and a brazier grill.

Foods pictured are, from left, Hickory Beef Rib Roast, Foil Baked Potatoes, Barbecue Butter French Bread, Shish Kebob, Shrimp and Scollop Kebobs, Pineapple Glazed Ham, Hawaiian Baked Beans, Corn In Foil, Cheddar Dogs and Tournedo Burgers. See recipes in index.

Hickory Chips & Garlic Buds — that's the secret to Chef Bell's unique method of flavoring red meat roasts. At left, wet hickory wood chips and buds of fresh garlic are placed among hot charcoal briquets for covered cooking of Hickory Beef Rib Roast. The same delicate hickory flavor can be imparted to Rolled Lamb Shoulder, above, or Rolled Pork Loin, below. Note correct use of foil drip pan and spacing of charcoal for covered roasting. See recipes.

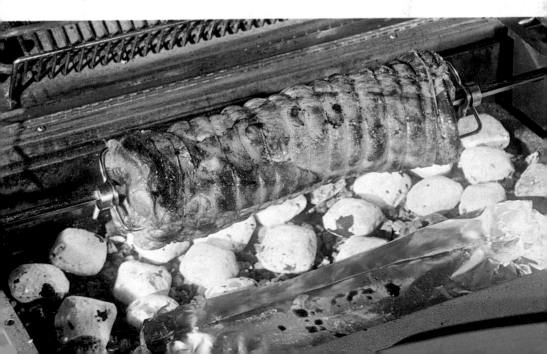

Variety is what makes charcoal cooking so intriguing to the barbecue enthusiast. As a start, he can draw from a wide selection of reliable basic meat recipes, such as Grilled Spareribs (lamb or pork), above, Shish Kebob or Grilled Lamb Chops, below. With experience, recipes take on a "personalized" touch through use of marinades and basting sauces. Soon ordinary fare becomes a colorful patio "spectacular" like Barbecued Chicken Parts cooked with Wine Basting Sauce, at left. See recipes.

Barbecued turkey is an all-American favorite, especially when charcoal cooked to an aromatic rich brown. No other cooking method holds in the natural juices better, or adds so much to the delicate flavor of turkey. Above is Spit-Roasted Whole Turkey, cooked with Oriental Basting Sauce. At left, Spit-Barbecued Turkey Roll, is a modern winner every time if cooked over charcoal. See recipes.

The American Favorite

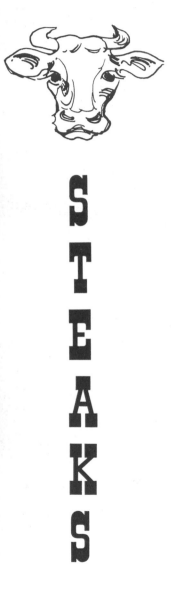

STEAKS

Charcoal cooking steaks has become an American leisuretime tradition, whether in the back yard on a Sunday afternoon, or away on an outing. Easy, tasty and fun to prepare, Barbecued Steak is one of the really elegant foods which require no fancy fixings or culinary skill. A first attempt can be a sure success by following Chef Bell's instructions in Basic Grilled Steaks. See recipe.

Sunday Afternoon Steaks

Charcoal Broiled Steaks   Tossed Green Salad

Hot Garlic French Bread

Coffee   or Soft Drinks

Kebobs, like colors from an artist's palette, can be blended in infinite variety from a handfull of basic ingredients. Here is where the barbecue artist can really show off. Above, the traditional Shish Kebob of marinated lamb, plus some fruit and vegetable variations. Below, a rich fruit sauce glazes Hawaiian Lamb Kebobs. At right, a party hors d'oeuvre setting of tomatoes, ham, potato fritters and pineapple. And this is just a start! See recipes.

Garnish is an important part of fine barbecue cooking. While beautifully grilled, the lamb ribs and burger above make a far more attractive serving topped with Grilled Pineapple Rings. Most meat courses require some garnish, a sprinkling of paprika, slices of tomato, pepper, onion, mushrooms, olives and the like. Most fresh or canned fruits will do — though flavors should complement the entree. And remember lots of fresh green parsley, the universal barbecue garnish.

The choice spencer steaks above, though expertly cooked, need a garnish of contrasting color. Small Vegetable Kebobs on the grill will be a colorful garnish as well as a vegetable entree. Below, the franks on a skewer, Beef Kebobs and Rolled Beef Roast all have eye-appealing colors of their own. For contrast, the refreshing green of lime punch completes the setting.

Picnics have become gourmet meal treats with the appearance of modern barbecue techniques, portable equipment and new cooking aids. Handy aluminum foil has revolutionized charcoal cooking, from Foil Burgers, above, to Foil Baked Potatoes and Corn, below, which will be roasted right in the coals under Chicken & Barbecue Sauce. See recipes and Foil Cooking chapter.

Seafood becomes something special when charcoal cooked. Whether saltwater, freshwater, fishing line-fresh or frozen, barbecue cooking seals in juices and imparts outdoor goodness to all seafood. Pictured above are, Foil Steamed Clams, Fresh Grilled Trout, Barbecued Split Lobster, Scallop and Shrimp Kebobs, Grilled Salmon and Halibut Steaks and a Grill Steamed Crab. See Recipes.

Barbecue cooking can be as informal or sophisticated as the occasion. Many of the world's leading restaurants require charcoal cookery for gourmet cuisine. You can too! Consider this Spit-Roasted Fresh Ham with Fruit Jelly Glaze and Grilled Pineapple Rings. What could be more appropriate for an elegant table setting? See recipes.

VEGETABLES & FRUIT

Vegetables are easily cooked on the barbecue using heavy duty foil.

FRENCH GRILLED TOMATOES

3 large, solid beefsteak
   tomatoes
4 tsp. parsley, chopped
1 tsp. garlic salt

4 tsp. butter, melted
6 tsp. grated Parmesan
   cheese (or bread
    crumbs)

Wash and cut tomatoes in half. Place cut side up on double thick heavy-duty aluminum foil. Brush each tomato half with melted butter, sprinkle about ¼ tsp. of garlic salt on each and a generous sprinkling of Parmesan cheese (or bread crumbs), top off with parsley. Wrap foil edges securely and place about 4 to 5-inches above coals 10 to 15 minutes, just long enough to heat tomatoes through. Leave foil open at top when cooking in covered unit. Serve immediately.

MUSHROOMS IN FOIL

½ lb. fresh mushrooms,
   whole or sliced
1½ tbs. butter
Dash of salt

Dash of monosodium
   glutamate
1 tbs. sherry wine
   (optional)

Wash and rinse mushrooms well; place on heavy-duty aluminum foil. Dot with butter and seasonings. Wrap edges securely, put on grill over hot coals for 15 to 20 minutes. Serve with barbecued steak, roast or scrambled eggs.

FOIL BAKED POTATOES

Select even-sized baking potatoes and scrub well in cold water with a brush. Puncture skins a few times with knife point to prevent potato from bursting. Rub well with butter or oil and sprinkle liberally with salt. Wrap securely in double weight foil, dull side out. Place potatoes among coals and bake 30 to 40 minutes, turning each 5 minutes ¼ turn with tongs. Potatoes are done when they feel soft inside when squeezed with tongs. To serve, cut through top of foil wrapper and "fluff" potato by pushing in from ends or with a fork. Top with butter, parsley and seasonings of your choice. Note: For cooking on grill, over hot coals, allow an additional 10 to 20 minutes of cooking time. Turn as usual.

FROZEN POTATOES IN FOIL

Any of the frozen potatoes such as potato fritters, French fries, shredded potatoes, etc., can be wrapped securely in heavy-duty aluminum foil with 1 tbs. butter, salt and pepper to taste and grilled 4 to 5-inches above hot coals for about 25 minutes, until foil package is soft when pinched with tongs. Turn once or twice. Open foil package on top and continue to cook a few minutes longer to crisp potatoes.

FOIL BAKED YAMS

Select even sized yams or sweet potatoes and follow directions for Foil Baked Potatoes. Foil packets may be opened after yams are soft and a mixture of butter and brown sugar or honey added. Cook a few minutes longer to glaze. Serve in foil wrappers.

YUMMY BAKED BEANS

3 1-lb. cans (6 cups) pork and beans in tomato. sauce	1 tbs. Worcestershire sauce
1 tbs. wine vinegar	¾ cup catsup
1 tbs. soy sauce	10 slices of smoked bacon, cut in small pieces

Empty one can of beans into a large casserole or all-metal pan. Combine seasoning ingredients and sprinkle one-third of the mixture over the beans. Repeat for second and third can of beans. Place casserole on grill over coals and, if an open unit, cover loosely with foil. Leave casserole uncovered. For covered units, this will allow the charcoal (hickory chip and garlic, if desired) flavor to penetrate into the beans as they cook. Cook 45 minutes for covered units, 1 hour for open grills.

SWEET POTATO — PINEAPPLE KEBOBS

Parboil scrubbed sweet potatoes. Cool and remove peelings, cut into cubes, salt lightly. Alternate on skewers with fresh or canned pineapple chunks. Brush with melted butter (brown sugar may be added if desired). Grill over hot coals until browned on all sides, about 20 minutes.

ONION-POTATO BAKE

½ cup butter or margarine
    softened
1 envelope onion-soup mix

6 baking potatoes,
    scrubbed

Cut each potato in 4 lengthwise slices. Blend butter with soup mix and spread on slices, then reassemble potato. Place on sheet of aluminum foil and wrap completely. Place on grill or among hot coals. Bake 40 to 50 minutes. Serve with additional butter.

HUSKED CORN IN FOIL

Remove corn husks and silk, rinse well in cold water. Place cob on heavy-duty aluminum foil and spread with 1 tbs. butter and sprinkle with about 2 tbs. water. Wrap foil securely and lay on coals about 20 mins., turning every 5 minutes. If cooked on grill, allow 40 minutes.

CORN ON THE COALS

Remove the large outer husks from corn; turn back inner husks, remove silk and rinse well in cold water. Spread corn with softened butter and salt lightly. Replace husks over ears, twist ends or tie with fine wire. Roast on grill over hot coals. Turn every 5 minutes until done, 15 to 20 minutes. Serve hot with more salt, pepper and butter.

CORN IN FOIL

Follow above directions — except rewrap corn in husks then in aluminum foil and lay on coals about 20 mins., turning every 5 minutes. If cooked on grill, allow 40 minutes.

GRILLED ONION SLICES

Slice four large onions into ¾-inch slices and soak in French dressing for about 15 minutes. Place in barbecue basket or on grill and brown on both sides, about 3 to 5 minutes each side. Baste with French dressing occasionally. Serve with any red meat.

BAKED ACORN SQUASH

Cut squash in half, remove seeds and fiber. Brush inside and outside well with melted butter or margarine. Add a sprinkling of lemon juice; season to taste with salt and pepper. If desired, add a dash of nutmeg. Wrap each half of squash in double thick aluminum foil. Bake on grill until tender, about 45 minutes.

BAKED SUMMER SQUASH

Wash and pare squash (crook-neck or zucchini) and cut into bite-size pieces. Place single serving portions in double thickness of aluminum foil and sprinkle with Herb Butter (see recipe) and salt. Close edges of foil package tightly and place on grill or directly on coals. Cook 30 to 40 minutes, turning each 10 minutes. Serve topped with the butter and juice from the foil package.

VARIATIONS: Add spiced tomato sauce, barbecue sauce, chunks of fresh tomato, onion, celery, garlic, Parmesan cheese or bread crumbs.

BARBECUED STUFFED PEPPERS

Cut tops from large green peppers and remove seeds. Rinse well and fill with a mixture of chili and beans, seasoned with bits of cheese and topped with catsup. Wrap each pepper in a double thickness of heavy-duty foil, securely folding edges. Cook on grill, over hot coals 30 to 40 minutes, turning occasionally, or place among coals for 30 minutes, turning often. Just before serving, open foil and top each pepper with additional cheese.

VARIATIONS: Use straight chili, cooked meat mixtures, cooked Spanish rice or cheese and rice mixture.

MIXED VEGETABLE KEBOBS

6 small potatoes	¼ cup melted butter
6 small onions	2 tsp. barbecue spice
12 large fresh mushrooms	1 tsp. salt
2 green peppers	¼ tsp. black pepper
	6 small tomatoes

Pare and cook potatoes in boiling salted water until tender but not soft. Do the same with the onions. Cut stems off mushrooms, wash caps. Remove seeds and cut peppers into 12 pieces. Drain potatoes and onions and arrange on 6 skewers alternately with peppers and mushroom caps. Mix together melted butter, barbecue spice, salt and pepper and brush kebobs with mixture. Cook over grill until lightly browned, about 5 minutes. Add tomato to each, turn and baste, cook 5 minutes longer. Makes 6 kebobs.

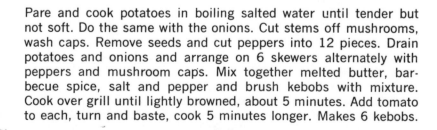

VEGETABLE KEBOBS FOR GARNISH

Use very short skewers or butcher's wooden meat skewers. Select vegetables which will complement the meat course (such as peppers, tomatoes, mushrooms, etc., for beef and poultry — parboiled sweet potatoes, onions, peppers etc., for pork and lamb) and alternate 2 or three pieces of each on each skewer. Brush with butter and grill over medium coals 3 to 5 minutes on each side, or until lightly browned. Season with salt and pepper and serve with meat entree for flavorful garnish.

GREEN BEANS 'N MUSHROOMS

1 pkg. (12-oz.) frozen French cut green beans
2 tbs. butter or margarine
¼ cup sliced fresh mushrooms (or 1 small can sliced mushrooms)

⅛ tsp. monosodium glutamate
½ tsp. salt
Pepper
1 to 2 tbs. green onions, chopped

Place green beans on double thickness of heavy-duty foil. Add mushrooms and remaining ingredients, and wrap edges securely. Cook on coals 10 to 20 minutes, or on grill 30 to 40 minutes, turning 2 or 3 times. When ready to serve, place in serving dish and top with butter.

BARBECUED FROZEN VEGETABLES

FROZEN VEGETABLES IN FOIL

Place frozen vegetables on square of double layer aluminum foil, dot with butter or margarine, sprinkle with salt and dash of pepper and monosodium glutamate. To these vegetables you may add a pinch of herbs or spices, or chopped chives or onions. Close foil edges securely and cook on grill or place down in or around the ash-grey coals. Turn once or twice with tongs during cooking. The following chart lists approximate grill cooking time:

40 to 50 Minutes

Peas	Broccoli
Spinach	Brussels Sprouts
Limas, large	Squash
Whole Kernel Corn	Green Beans

50 to 60 Minutes

Asparagus	Mixed Vegetables
Cauliflower	Peas and Carrots
Limas, small	Succotash

NOTE: For rich barbecue flavor, open foil packet during final 5 minutes of cooking to allow fumes to reach vegetables.

LIMA MUSHROOM CASSEROLE

2 pkgs. frozen lima beans, cooked	½ cup Italian style tomato sauce
1 can cream of mushroom soup	1 tbs. green chili peppers, chopped (or ¼ tsp. chili powder)
1 cup water (or 1 cup white or red wine)	3 tbs. brown sugar

Pour drained lima beans into casserole. Dilute mushroom soup with water and add. Stir in remaining ingredients and cook uncovered for about 30 minutes on back of grill over medium coals.

CALIFORNIA BAKED BEANS

1 1-lb. can baked beans	3 tbs. orange juice concentrate
1 tbs. molasses	

In heavy skillet or casserole, combine all ingredients mixing well. Cover, set on back of grill stirring occasionally until hot (20 to 30 minutes). Remove cover during last 5 minutes of cooking.

MIXED BEAN POT

1 Bermuda onion, finely chopped	½ cup hickory catsup or regular catsup
1 clove garlic, minced	¼ cup cold water or red wine
3 slices of bacon, chopped	3 tbs. vinegar
1 1-lb. can baked beans, tomato-style	2 tbs. brown sugar or molasses
1 1-lb. can garbanzo beans, drained	1 tsp. dry mustard
1 1-lb. can red kidney beans	1 to 2 tsp. salt
	Pepper

In a skillet on the grill, brown bacon, add onion and garlic, cooking until golden. Add remaining ingredients stirring well. When heated thoroughly, cover and simmer for about 30 minutes, stirring occasionally. Uncover during final 5 minutes.

CHUCK WAGON BEAN POT

2 large cans baked beans	½ tsp. barbecue sauce
⅓ cup catsup	½ tsp. monosodium glutamate
¼ cup molasses	
2 tsp. brown sugar	½ tsp. onion salt
2 tsp. dry mustard	4 slices bacon, cooked

Mix together all ingredients, except bacon in a heavy pot. Cut bacon strips in half and place on top of beans. Cover, set on back of grill and cook stirring occasionally for about 30 minutes or until beans are hot.

GRILLED FRUIT GARNISHES

In addition to pineapple rings and apples, other fruits such as pears, oranges, grapefruit, peaches, nectarines, papayas, melons and bananas may be sliced and grilled quickly for garnishes.

GRILLED APPLE RINGS

Slice cored apples into ½-inch rings. Brush with butter and sprinkle with brown sugar and cinnamon. Grill 4 inches from coals about 5 minutes per side, or until lightly browned. Serve as meat garnish or hot fruit entree.

SPICED APPLES

4 to 6 baking apples	½ cube butter
½ cup brown sugar, maple syrup or honey	2 tsp. cinnamon
	½ cup raisins (optional)

Wash and core apples. Place each on a double thickness of heavy-duty foil. Add about 1 tsp. butter then fill centers with mixture of 2 tbs. sugar (maple syrup or honey), ¼ tsp. cinnamon and top with few raisins (if desired), and another teaspoon of butter. Wrap edges of foil securely and cook right side up 45 minutes to 1 hour on grill, or 25 to 35 minutes on coals. Apples are done when soft. Serve topped with whipped cream or scoop of vanilla ice cream if using grilled apples for a dessert. Excellent garnish for pork.

GRILLED PINEAPPLE RINGS

Drain canned pineapple rings and dry on paper towel. Brush with butter or oil and lay on grill 3 inches from coals. Cook only until lightly browned on both sides. Serve as garnish for meats or as a tasty hot fruit entree. Colorful decoration for ham, pork or lamb, with a red cherry or apricot piece in ring center.

HONEY PINEAPPLE WEDGES

1 fresh pineapple   **3 tbs. honey or brown sugar**

Remove top but do not peel pineapple. Cut into six or eight length-wise wedges, remove center core. Place in oblong pan, spoon honey or brown sugar over fruit and marinate 45 minutes to 1 hour. Turn occasionally to thoroughly coat pineapple. Place pineapple skin-side down on grill 3 to 5 inches from hot coals. Grill 10 to 20 minutes, or until pineapple is steaming hot. Serve immediately with spareribs, pork chops, pork roast or ham.

FRUIT KEBOBS

Prepare a variety of fresh or canned fruits in chunks of same size such as, pineapple, papaya, apple, firm cooked pitted prunes, peaches, bananas, pears, maraschino cherries, orange quarters, dried apricots etc. Thread fruit along skewers alternating chunks and brush with honey thinned with lemon juice (about 1 cup honey to 2 tbs. lemon juice). Oil grill to prevent sticking. Grill fruit kebobs over hot coals, brushing with butter occasionally. Turn frequently to prevent scorching. Serve with remaining honey mixture, as entree or garnish for meats and poultry.

GREAT GRILLED GRAPEFRUIT

3 grapefruit
¼ cup honey or brown
   sugar

¼ cup sherry wine
   (optional)
6 maraschino cherries

Cut grapefruit in halves and pare, loosening sections and removing seeds. Place each half on heavy-duty aluminum foil and spoon about 1 tsp. honey and 1 tsp. sherry wine over each grapefruit half. Place cherry in center and wrap foil securely around fruit. Cook on grill, cut side up, 15 to 20 minutes. Serve for breakfast, appetizer or dessert.

CHOCOLATE BANANA BOAT

Peel a firm banana. Cut out a V-shaped wedge lengthwise and fill the groove with chocolate chips (or chopped almond-chocolate candy bar). Top with marshmallow bits. Lay banana wedge back in place, wrap tightly in foil. Grill 5 to 10 minutes.

BANANA HONEYS

4 to 6 firm bananas

¼ cup honey

Make a lengthwise slit in peel of banana with sharp knife. Loosen peel about 1-inch on either side of slit. Spoon 1 tbs. of honey along fruit, close peel. Cook on grill over hot coals until banana peel turns glossy black and fruit is soft, about 8 to 12 minutes. Excellent served as meat accompaniment, dessert or as hot breakfast fruit.

Sandwiches & Breads
Burger Bonanza

BASIC GRILLED BURGERS

1½ lbs. ground meat (beef or lamb)
¾ tsp. salt
Dash of pepper (optional)
1 tsp. monosodium glutamate

Lightly mix all ingredients, and shape into 6 patties. (The less they're handled, the tastier and jucier they will be.) Broil on grill over hot coals, turning once, about 10 minutes or until nicely browned. Serve in hot buttered hamburger buns.

VARIATIONS:

CHEESE BURGERS

Follow basic recipe and top each patty with a slice of American, cheddar or jack cheese shortly after turning. Cheese should be lightly melted when burger is done.

SWISS BURGERS

Follow Cheese Burgers variation substituting a slice or two of Swiss cheese for topping.

HICKORY BURGERS

Add ¼ tsp. hickory smoke flavoring to basic recipe, or substitute smoke flavored salt in Basic recipe. Or, toss wet hickory chips among coals while cooking to impart flavor.

JUICY BURGERS

Add ½ cup evaporated milk to meat before shaping patties. If desired, season with minced onion or stir in 2 tbs. steak sauce.

EXPANDED BURGERS

Add ⅓ cup quick rolled oats, ½ cup evaporated milk and 2 tsp. Worcestershire to meat.

BACON CHEESE BURGERS

Add 3 slices grilled crisp diced bacon and ⅓ cup grated cheddar cheese to meat.

HERB BURGERS

Add to Basic recipe, ½ tsp. crushed herb (one only) such as basil, marjoram, oregano, tarragon, rosemary or sage. Grill as usual and serve with Herb Butter (see recipe) made with the same herb as is in meat, brushed over patties or onto toasted buns.

NUTTY BURGERS

Lightly mix about ½ cup dry cereal such as corn flakes, ½ cup chopped nuts, peanuts, cashews or walnuts, and ½ cup milk into meat before shaping.

PEANUT BUTTER BURGERS

Omit salt, pepper and m.s.g. called for in Basic recipe. Add to meat: ¼ cup crunchy-style peanut butter, ½ tsp. seasoned salt, a dash of seasoned pepper and 1 small grated onion.

SURPRISE BURGERS

Instead of 6, make 12 thin patties, following Basic recipe. Just before grilling, sandwich rounds of American cheese and/or pickle relish, or rounds of smoky cheese and thin onion slices between each two patties, seal edges well, and grill as usual.

ROQUEFORT OR BLEU BURGERS

Make patties as usual. After grilling one side, turn and spread cooked side with commercial cream-style bleu or roquefort cheese dressing. Continue broiling until bottom is done and dressing is hot.

BURGUNDY BURGERS

Add ¼ cup burgundy or other dry red table wine to Basic recipe, blending well before grilling.

BEER BURGERS

Add ¼ cup beer to Basic recipe, blending well before grilling.

FRANK BURGERS

Make burgers as in Basic recipe, but add 3 frankfurters, thinly sliced into rounds and ¼ cup evaporated milk to raw meat before grilling.

STROGANOFF BURGERS

Omit salt from Basic recipe and prepare as usual, adding ¼ cup commercial sour cream, 1 tbs. minced parsley, ⅛ tsp. oregano, and ¾ tsp. garlic salt.

INDIA BURGERS

Follow Basic recipe and add ½ tsp. curry powder to meat. Grill as usual and serve on buns with sliced banana rounds, chutney, chopped peanuts and chopped onions.

ITALIAN BURGERS

Mix 1 tbs. dry spaghetti sauce mix into Basic recipe and grill. Sprinkle with grated mozzarella cheese before slipping into buns.

MEXICAN BURGERS

Add ¼ cup grated cheese, ¼ cup tomato juice and 1 tsp. chili powder to Basic recipe and prepare as usual. Serve with Mexican Salsa Sauce (see recipe).

FRENCH BURGERS

Add ½ tsp. mixed herbs and 2 tsp. dry Vermouth to Basic recipe. Prepare as usual, serve on rounds of French Bread.

ORIENTAL BURGERS

Add 2 tbs. chopped fresh mushrooms, ¼ tsp. ground ginger, 1 tsp. soy sauce and 1 tsp. sugar to basic recipe and prepare as usual.

HAWAIIAN BURGERS

Add 1 tsp. instant onion and 2 tbs. pineapple preserve to Basic recipe. Grill and serve with lightly grilled pineapple slices on each burger.

MUSHROOM BURGERS

Add ¼ cup chopped fresh or canned mushrooms to Basic recipe or place large fresh buttered mushrooms on grill along with meat, turning at the same time and serving atop meat patty. Garnish with sprigs of parsley.

DELUXE CHEESEBURGERS

2 lb. ground beef or
   lamb
1 tsp. salt
½ tsp. celery seed
Dash of pepper
½ cup tomato juice

⅔ cup stuffed green
   olives, chopped
3 tbs. chopped fresh
   parsley
2 tbs. chopped onion
1 egg
6 slices American cheese

Mix all ingredients except cheese, shape into 6 patties and grill over hot coals. When done, place a slice of cheese on each patty.

NUTTY FRUIT BURGERS

1 lb. ground beef or
   lamb
¼ cup chopped almonds,
   cashews or pecans
1 small onion, grated
1 tsp. salt
⅛ tsp. ground cloves

½ cup canned peaches,
   apricots or pears, mashed
1 tbs. brown sugar
2 tsp. cider vinegar
⅛ tsp. ground ginger
½ tsp. monosodium
   glutamate

Mix the ground beef lightly with nuts, onion, salt, cloves and 3 tbs. of the fruit. Shape into patties ½ to 1-inch thick. Place on greased grill over medium hot coals. Brush with a sauce made of the remaining fruit seasoned with brown sugar, vinegar, ginger and monosodium glutamate. Grill about 4 to 8 minutes on each side, or until nicely browned. Serve on toasted bun with pickles.

APPLESAUCE-NUT BURGERS

2 lbs. ground beef, or
   lamb
1 onion, grated
1 egg
⅔ cup canned applesauce
1 tsp. salt
¼ tsp. pepper

8 hamburger buns,
   toasted and buttered
½ cup (1 cube) butter
   or margarine
1 cup chopped nuts
1 tsp. seasoned salt

Combine ground meat, onion, egg, applesauce and seasonings. Shape into 8 thick patties. Grill about 8 minutes on each side over hot coals, or until done. Meanwhile, saute nuts in butter and seasoned salt. Stir often and cook about 5 minutes. When meat is done, place in buns and spoon nut mixture over each patty and serve immediately.

LAMBWICHES

1 lb. ground lean lamb	¼ cup celery, finely
1 tsp. garlic salt	chopped
Dash of pepper	¼ tsp. oregano
	(optional)

Thoroughly mix all ingredients and shape into 8 finger-shaped rolls about 4-inches long. Cook on greased grill over hot coals about 15 minutes, browning all sides. Serve in frankfurter rolls.

GENUINE BARBECUE SANDWICHES

Cut hot barbecued meat or poultry into very thin slices. Place in a double-thick sheet of heavy duty foil and turn up edges. Pour over a half and half mixture of Basic Barbecue Sandwich Sauce (see recipe) and natural cooking juices (from drip pan) and place foil package on the grill with the top opened. As soon as the sauce bubbles slightly, remove from grill and serve in warmed French rolls or sour dough bread. A slice of cheese may be added for additional flavor. Note: If natural cooking juices are not available, use bouillon.

Hot Dog Bonanza

ALL AMERICAN HOT DOG (Basic Recipe)

6 wieners or franks	6 hot dog buns
	Butter

Place franks on grill and cook 3 to 5 minutes per side over medium coals. Frequent turning with tongs will prevent curling. During the last minute, place split and buttered buns face-down on grill to toast. Slip browned wieners into buns and serve with any combination of pickle relish, mustard, catsup, onions, chopped tomatoes and shredded lettuce.

VARIATIONS:

BACON DOGS

Wrap franks with a strip of bacon, securing with a pick. Grill until bacon is crisp, turning often. Remove pick before serving.

CHEDDAR DOGS

Slit each frank lengthwise almost through and lay in a strip of aged cheddar cheese. Lay on grill, cheese up, cover lightly with foil and cook until frank is hot and cheese melted. No turning required.

CHILI DOGS

Follow Basic Recipe, topping hot dog with a generous spoonful of heated canned chili or brick chili. Sprinkle with chopped onions.

PINEAPPLE DOGS

Slit each frank almost through lengthwise and fill opening with a strip of pineapple. Wrap with bacon, secure with wooden picks and grill until bacon is crisp on all sides. Remove pick before serving.

SAUERKRAUT DOGS

Slit each frank almost through lengthwise and fill opening with caraway sprinkled sauerkraut. Wrap entirely with bacon, secure with wooden pick and grill until bacon is crisp, turning often. Remove pick before serving.

TACO DOGS

Grill franks until hot. Roll up in tortillas, seasoned with taco or barbecue sauce (a little shredded lettuce, cheese or chopped tomato may be included). Secure tortilla with pick. Return to grill, turning with tongs until tortilla is hot. A little butter or oil may be brushed on tortillas while turning for crisp outside. Serve with additional sauce and beans.

HAWAIIAN FRANK KEBOBS

Cut franks into thirds and alternate on skewers with chunks of pineapple, green pepper or onions (both optional). Grill over medium coals until lightly browned, turning often. Kebobs may be flavored during cooking by basting with Sweet & Sour Baste (see recipe).

FRANK KEBOBS

Slice franks in thirds, and thread on skewers with large slices of dill pickle and slices of small onion. Broil until the franks are well browned, and serve in toasted hot dog buns, with mustard if desired, or as appetizers.

BARBECUED SEASONED BREADS

Cut a large loaf of French bread or sour-dough bread in half lengthwise, through the side. Spread with any of the Seasoned Butter Recipes. Sprinkle with additional grated parmesan cheese and paprika, if desired, and wrap each half in heavy duty foil, dull side out. Place on grill 4 to 6 inches above medium coals and heat 10 to 15 minutes, turning once or twice. Open foil during final minutes of cooking for added charcoal flavor. Note: Whole loaves may be cooked, halves together, in the same package if foil is wrapped loosely. Always keep warm right up to serving time.

PARMESAN FRENCH BREAD

1 loaf French bread
½ cup mayonnaise
¼ cup butter, softened
½ cup Parmesan cheese

¼ cup onion, finely chopped (optional)
½ tsp. Worchestershire sauce
Paprika

Cut loaf of French in half lengthwise, spread cut surfaces with butter. Mix remaining ingredients together, except paprika and spread on bread, sprinkle with paprika. Put bread halves together on large piece of foil, wrapping securely. Place on grill 10 to 20 minutes. Cut bread crosswise to serve.

BISCUITS ON A STICK

Cut commercial refrigerated biscuits into thirds or halves and thread on skewer, leaving a little space between each. Bake over hot coals about 7 minutes, or until completely done, turning often to brown all sides. Brush with melted butter.

VARIATIONS:

GARLIC BISCUITS: After cooking, brush with a mixture of melted butter and garlic salt.

PARSLEY BISCUITS: Brush baked biscuits with Parsley Butter (see recipe).

CHEESE & CHIVE BISCUITS: Brush each baked biscuit with a mixture made of melted butter and canned grated American or parmesan cheese. Sprinkle with finely chopped chives.

CINNAMON BUNS: Brush cooked biscuits with melted butter, and sprinkle with cinnamon flavored sugar.

SEASONINGS

Delicate flavoring is imparted to barbecued foods with a basting sauce, applied during cooking.

Marinades & Cooking Sauces

BASIC POULTRY MARINADE

½ cup olive oil or salad oil
⅓ cup dry white wine
¼ cup white wine vinegar
1 clove garlic, crushed
1 tsp. dry mustard

½ tsp. poultry seasoning
½ tsp. celery salt
1 tsp. salt
¼ tsp. black pepper
½ tsp. monosodium glutamate

Blend all ingredients well and pour over poultry. Let stand 2 to 3 hours, turning several times. Brush each piece of fowl each time before turning over while barbecuing. Baste every 20 minutes for poultry on spit or in spit basket.

HERBED CHICKEN MARINADE

½ cup olive oil
Juice of 1 lemon
¼ cup white wine
2 tbs. onion, minced
1 clove garlic, minced
¼ tsp. rosemary

¼ tsp. tarragon
¼ tsp. thyme
1 tsp. salt
Dash of pepper
Dash of monosodium
  glutamate

Blend all ingredients well. Marinate chicken at room temperature for 2 to 3 hours before cooking. Use marinade to baste chicken during barbecuing.

VERMOUTH POULTRY MARINADE

Combine 1 cup sweet or dry vermouth (depending on your taste), with ¾ cup olive oil and ½ tsp. salt. Blend well and marinate chicken, turkey or game for at least 2 hours before cooking. Use remaining liquid as basting sauce.

MINT MARINADE

2 tbs. mint leaves,
  minced (or dried mint
  leaves)
⅓ cup olive oil, or
  salad oil
1 cup dry white wine
1 clove garlic, mashed

¼ tsp. basil, crushed
¼ tsp. freshly ground
  black pepper
1 tbs. parsley, minced
  (fresh or dried)
1 tsp. sugar
½ tsp. salt

Blend all ingredients well. Pour over cubed lamb and marinate 2 to 3 hours. Also good for chicken. Makes about 1 ½ cups of marinade.

MARINADE FOR GAME

⅔ cup salad oil
⅓ cup dry red wine
2 tbs. minced onions or
  shallots
1 clove garlic, minced
1 tbs. juniper berries,
  mashed (or ¼ tsp.
  allspice or cloves)

½ tsp. coarse ground
  pepper
1 bay leaf
½ tsp. thyme
1 tsp. salt

Blend all ingredients well. Pour over game (such as rabbit or venison), and marinate in refrigerator 1 or 2 days. Turn twice a day. Use remaining marinade to baste meat while barbecuing. Recipe makes 1 cup of marinade.

HERBED LAMB MARINADE

1 cup olive oil
½ cup wine vinegar
1 clove garlic, mashed
1 tsp. dried mint
½ tsp. thyme
½ tsp. oregano

½ tsp. monosodium
  glutamate
1 tsp. freshly ground
  pepper
1 tsp. salt

Combine all ingredients and blend well. Marinate lamb for at least 2 hours or overnight before barbecuing. While meat is cooking baste frequently with marinade. Makes about 1⅔ cups, enough for 6 chops or a 3 to 5 pound lamb roast.

SHISH KEBOB MARINADE

¾ cup dry white wine
½ cup olive oil (or
  salad oil
2 cloves minced garlic
1 tsp. oregano

1 tsp. basil
¼ tsp. onion salt
½ tsp. salt
⅛ tsp. pepper

Blend all ingredients. Recipe makes enough for 2 to 2½ lbs. cubed lamb.

ROYALE LAMB MARINADE

¾ cube butter or
  margarine
2 small cloves garlic,
  minced (or ½ tsp.
  garlic salt)
1½ tsp. salt

2 tsp. monosodium
  glutamate
¼ tsp. coarse-ground
  pepper
1 tbs. lemon juice

Cream butter together with remaining ingredients. Spread over rolled shoulder of lamb, coating completely. Let stand in the refrigerator until you are ready to spit-barbecue. The marinade serves as a self-basting sauce while the lamb cooks.

TERIYAKI MARINADE

½ cup soy sauce
¼ cup sherry wine
2 tbs. brown sugar
1¼ tsp. dry mustard

1 clove garlic, crushed
1 tbs. fresh ground gin-
  ger (or ½ tsp. ginger
  powder)

Mix all ingredients together until sugar is dissolved. Pour into a shallow dish large enough to hold either meat or chicken. Marinate for at least 1 hour (longer if possible), turning pieces at least two or three times. Drain before cooking on grill. Use marinade to baste during barbecuing of pork, beef, lamb and poultry.

SPARERIBS MARINADE

1 cup orange juice
½ cup honey
½ cup soy sauce
¼ cup water
1 cup wine or cider
    vinegar

1 tsp. dry mustard
1 tsp. paprika
1 clove garlic, crushed
Dash of Tabasco sauce
¼ tsp. allspice

Blend all ingredients well. Good 1 hour marinade and basting sauce for spareribs, chicken and ham. Makes about 3½ cups.

SHERRY 'N SPICE MARINADE

½ cup sherry wine
¼ cup salad oil
1 medium onion, grated
2 tsp. Worcestershire
    sauce
1 tbs. dry mustard
¾ tsp. dried herbs, such
    as marjoram, rose-
    mary, oregano, thyme

½ tsp. garlic salt
⅛ tsp. salt
½ tsp. fresh ground
    black pepper
¼ tsp. monosodium
    glutamate

Combine all ingredients in jar and shake well, blend thoroughly, Use as a marinade for beef, veal, lamb or chicken. Use remaining marinade to baste during barbecuing.

SEAFOOD MARINADE

¼ cup oil
½ cup dry white wine
1 tsp. sugar
1 tbs. parsley, minced

1 tsp. paprika
½ tsp. salt
⅛ tsp. pepper

Blend all ingredients. Pour over seafood such as shrimp, scallops, lobster or almost any type fish. Makes a little over ¾ cups marinade, enough for 2 lbs. of seafood.

ALL PURPOSE BASTING SAUCE

⅔ cup olive or salad oil
⅓ cup fresh lemon juice
¼ cup soy sauce
⅓ cup wine vinegar
¼ cup tarragon vinegar

1 tsp. sugar
½ tsp. monosodium
   glatamate
Salt and pepper to taste

Mix all ingredients together and store in covered jar in refrigerator. Before using, shake thoroughly to mix.

SPANISH BASTING SAUCE

1 cup chopped Spanish
   onion
⅔ cup olive oil
¾ cup water
¾ cup catsup
⅓ cup lemon juice
4 tbs. sugar
4 tbs. Worcestershire

2 tbs. prepared mustard
2 tsp. salt
⅓ tsp. freshly ground
   pepper
¼ tsp. celery salt
1 tbs. fresh celery leaves,
   ground
¼ tsp. tobasco sauce

Saute onion in olive oil until tender. Just as the onion begins to turn brown, add the remaining ingredients and simmer for about 10 minutes. This sauce is good used as a basting sauce for chickens, turkeys, Cornish game hens, and for short ribs and hamburgers. It may also be served hot with the meat.

ORIENTAL BASTING SAUCE FOR TURKEY

1 6-oz. can frozen
   pineapple juice
¼ cup soy sauce
¼ cup brown sugar

¼ cup salad oil
2 tsp. salt
¼ tsp. black pepper

Blend all ingredients in small saucepan and cook over medium heat for 5 to 10 minutes or until sugar is dissolved. Makes enough basting sauce for a 6 to 12-lb. turkey. Use as basting sauce only during last 30 minutes of cooking time.

RED WINE MEAT SAUCE

1 cup dry red wine
1 cup olive oil
2 cloves garlic, crushed
½ tsp. each thyme and
   marjoram

1 tsp. rosemary
¼ cup parsley, finely
   minced
½ tsp. freshly ground
   black pepper

Combine all ingredients in large jar and shake thoroughly. Allow to stand at least 1 hour before using. Use as a marinade or for basting sauce for all red meats.

PORK BASTING SAUCE

Combine thoroughly ½ cup brown sugar (firmly packed), 4 tbs. honey and ¼ cup orange, pineapple or grapefruit juice, ¼ tsp. dry mustard. Use for basting pork during cooking.

SWEET & SOUR BASTE

1 cup crushed pineapple, undrained
⅔ cup white wine or chicken broth
2 tbs. white wine vinegar
2 tbs. peanut oil or salad oil
1 ½ tbs. soy sauce
1 tsp. lemon juice

¼ tsp. garlic salt (or minced garlic)
½ tsp. dry mustard
2 tbs. brown sugar
1 tbs. chopped onion (optional)
¼ tsp. monosodium glutamate

In saucepan, combine all ingredients mixing well and simmer 10 to 15 minutes. Use to brush baste over fish steaks, poultry, lamb, pork and ribs. Makes about 2 cups.

HONEY-CRANBERRY BASTE

1 cup cranberry sauce
¾ cup chicken broth
3 tbs. honey
2 tbs. green onions, chopped (optional)

2 tbs. salad oil
1 tsp. salt
1 tbs. wine vinegar
2 tbs. cornstarch

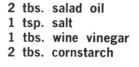

In saucepan, blend all ingredients well and simmer 10 to 15 minutes. Baste chicken, pork or turkey the last 20 minutes of cooking time. Heat remaining honey cranberry baste and serve with entree.

LAMB BASTING SAUCE

¾ cup dry sauterne or sherry wine
¼ cup olive oil
¼ cup wine vinegar
2 cloves garlic, minced

¼ cup chopped fresh parsley
1 tsp. mixed dried herbs
1½ tsp. salt
½ tsp. pepper

Blend all ingredients well and use for a basting sauce during cooking on your favorite cut of lamb.

WESTERN BARBECUE SAUCE

1 cup chili sauce	1 tsp. freshly ground
1 cup catsup	pepper
¼ cup Worcestershire	¼ cup wine vinegar
1 tsp. chili powder	¼ cup tarragon vinegar
2 dashes Tabasco	4 tbs. honey
1 tsp. mustard	½ cup water
1 tsp. salt	

Combine all ingredients and if desired, bring to boiling point. Cooking is not necessary; the sauce can be applied as soon as mixed. This sauce is very good when used as a basting sauce for ribs during the last few minutes of barbecuing. If sauce is too thick, thin with small amounts of water.

SEVILLE BARBECUE SAUCE

Rind of 1 orange, cut	¼ cup brown sugar
into small pieces	1 tbs. prepared mustard
Juice of 2 oranges	¼ tsp. tarragon
½ cup cider vinegar	

Blend orange juice, vinegar and brown sugar in saucepan over heat. Stir in remaining ingredients and heat almost to the boiling point (do not boil); simmer about 10 minutes, stirring occasionally. Strain before using. Good for roast duck, barbecued ham or pork roast, as last-minute basting or table sauce. Makes about 2 cups.

CURRY BARBECUE SAUCE

¼ cup butter or	3 tbs. milk
margarine	¼ chopped raw apple
2 cloves garlic, mashed	¼ tsp. salt
¼ cup onion, minced	½ cup beef stock or
½ to 1 tbs. curry	bouillon
powder	½ cup raisins (optional)

In sauce pan, melt butter, saute garlic and onions until golden. Add remaining ingredients (except stock and raisins), simmer about 10 minutes stirring often. Pour in stock and raisins, stir well and simmer about 30 minutes. Add more stock if sauce gets too thick. This curry sauce can be brushed on chicken or lamb. Makes about 1¾ cups.

GINGER BASTE FOR PORK

⅔ cup brown sugar,
  firmly packed
2 tbs. cornstarch
2 tsp. freshly grated ginger
  root (or ½ tsp. powder
  ginger)

2 cloves garlic, crushed
¼ cup wine vinegar
⅔ cup soy sauce
¼ tsp. monosodium
  glutamate

Combine ingredients thoroughly until sugar is dissolved, let stand for at least 1 hour to blend flavors before using. Stir well before brushing on pork during cooking.

CHICKEN BARBECUE SAUCE

⅓ cup olive oil
1 cup water
3 tbs. chopped Spanish
  onion
½ tsp. garlic puree or
  garlic liquid
2 tsp. sugar
1 tsp. salt

2 tsp. paprika
1 tsp. freshly ground
  pepper
⅓ tsp. dry mustard
1¼ tsp. Worcestershire
1¼ tsp. Tabasco
2 tbs. tarragon vinegar

Combine all ingredients and simmer about 25 minutes. Use as a basting sauce when grilling or spit barbecuing chicken.

RIB BARBECUE SAUCE

½ cup soy sauce
½ cup catsup
1 tbs. Worchestershire
3 dashes Tabasco
¾ cup water
¼ cup wine vinegar

¼ cup tarragon vinegar
1 tbs. sugar
1 tsp. salt
1 tsp. celery seed
1 tsp. brown sugar
¼ cup pineapple juice

Combine all ingredients and heat to boiling point. Simmer 30 minutes. This makes enough sauce to baste 4 pounds of loin back ribs.

ORANGE GLAZE

1 cup orange juice
½ cup honey
3 tbs. grated orange
  rind

½ tsp. onion powder or
  onion salt
½ cup brown sugar

Mix all ingredients and brush over poultry, lamb or pork during the final 20 to 30 minutes of cooking.

FRUIT JELLY GLAZE

1 cup bouillon
¼ cup cider vinegar
1 tsp. dry mustard

½ cup jelly (such as currant, guava, pineapple-orange)

Mix first three ingredients in saucepan. Blend in jelley, bring to boiling point (do not boil), simmer about 10 minutes, stirring occasionally. Fine basting sauce for spareribs, ham or pork roast. Makes about 1 ¾ cups.

APRICOT OR PEACH GLAZE

1 cup apricots or peaches
3 tbs. lemon juice
2 tbs. salad oil
¼ liquid smoke (optional)

½ tsp. salt
1 tsp. chopped chives or finely chopped green onion

Puree fruits or place in electric blender until smooth. Add remaining ingredients in saucepan and simmer 8 to 12 minutes. Makes about 1 ⅓ cups. Baste on barbecuing chicken, lamb or pork during last 20 minutes cooking time.

HICKORY CHIPS & GARLIC BUDS (Chef Bell's Secret Seasoning)

Select only small size (1 to 2 inch) Tennessee hickory chips, with the outside bark intact (see Seasoning Coals instructional chapter) and soak them several hours in cold water before using. Break open a fresh garlic clove and rub loose coverings from individual buds. The exact amount to use depends on the number of hardwood briquets to be used, cooking time and richness of flavor desired. Generally, start by tossing 2 to 4 chips and buds among the hot coals when cooking starts. Replenish one or two at a time when required, every 20 minutes or so for long covered recipes or spit cooking, more often for shorter cooking times and grill cooking. The flavor of hickory, garlic and charcoal blend for a unique "Hickory Barbecue" flavor, obtainable in no other seasoning method. Use for all meats, poultry, seafoood and casserole recipes. Note: if chips dry out and start to burn, remove from coals with tongs and resoak in water. Chips should only smoke slowly, releasing flavors. As many as 6 to 8 garlic buds may be tossed in at once for quick flavoring of steaks and grilled foods. A loose covering of heavy duty foil over the food will help hold in flavor: close lid on barrel and covered units.

CITRUS PEEL SPICE

Use orange, lemon or grapefruit peels tossed on charcoal for extra flavoring of meats, poultry, fish and etc., a thin strip or two every 10 minutes or so.

SEASONED BUTTERS:

LEMON BUTTER

Cream ¼ lb. softened butter with 2 tbs. lemon juice and ½ tsp. grated lemon rind. Serve over chicken, seafood, or vegetables. Melt for basting sauce.

HERB BUTTER

Cream ¼ lb. softened butter with ½ tsp. (one only) tarragon, oregano or thyme. Also may be made with rosemary for poultry. Serve on cooked vegetables, light meats, seafood and poultry. Melt for basting sauce.

GREEN BUTTER

Cream ¼ lb. softened butter with 1 tbs. each, finely minced chives or green onion tops and parsley. Serve with seafood (especially shellfish), vegetables and lamb. Melt for basting sauce.

SHALLOT BUTTER

Cream ¼ lb. butter with 2 tbs. chopped shallots, which have been lightly sauteed in 1 tbs. butter, along with ½ tsp. lemon juice. Serve on hot steaks, chops, seafood or vegetables. Melt for basting sauce.

SHERRY BUTTER

Cream ¼ lb. softened butter with 3 tbs. sherry wine. Serve with hot vegetables such as squash, sweet potatoes, yams or carrots. Excellent with sweetbreads, veal and oysters.

DILL BUTTER

Cream ¼ lb. softened butter with ½ tsp. dill salt (or ¼ tsp. ground dill seed and ¼ tsp. salt). Serve with seafood, vegetables, poultry or in hot grilled French bread. Melt for basting sauce.

ANCHOVY BUTTER

Cream ¼ lb. softened butter with 2 tbs. anchovy paste and ¼ tsp. lemon juice. Serve with or spread over seafood, especially grilled fish steaks.

GARLIC BUTTER

Cream ¼ lb. softened butter with ½ to 1 tsp. finely minced garlic (or ¼ to ½ tsp. garlic salt or powder). Serve with seafoods, lamb, vegetables or in hot grilled French bread. (Amount of garlic varies with individual taste and garlic product strength.) Melt for basting sauce.

VARIATION: Blend equal parts butter with prepared garlic spread.

BARBECUE BUTTER

Cream ¼ lb. softened butter with ¼ tsp. seasoned salt (or barbecue spice), ½ tsp. paprika and 2 tsp. parmesan cheese. Spread on seafood, poultry, steaks, potatoes and hot French bread.

HOT SAUCE BUTTER

Cream ¼ lb. softened butter with ¼ to ½ tsp. Tobasco or hot sauce (depending on taste) and 1 tsp. lemon juice. Serve with meats, poultry, seafood and vegetables.

DRAWN BUTTER

Melt ¼ lb. butter in a sauce pan and stir in 2 tbs. flour. When well blended, stir in 1 cup water and juice of 1 lemon. Bring to a boil and remove from heat. Add ¼ lb. additional butter and stir until smooth. Serve with seafoods and vegetables.

Table Sauces & Relishes

MUSHROOM STEAK SAUCE

1 cup fresh mushrooms, sliced	1 tsp. soy sauce
	¼ tsp. onion salt
⅔ cup buillon or broth	Pinch rosemary
3 drops Tobasco sauce	1½ tsp. corn starch

Blend all ingredients except mushrooms in a sauce pan and bring to a boil, stirring constantly. Add mushrooms, stir and cover. Cook 5 minutes over low heat, stirring a few times.

ED BELL'S STEAK SAUCE

3 tbs. olive oil
⅓ cup brown sugar
½ cup soy sauce
⅓ tsp. cracked pepper
1 tsp. puree of garlic
   or juice from 2
   cloves garlic)

1 tsp. Worcestershire
Dash Tobasco
1 small piece ginger root
   (or 1 small piece
   ginger, grated)

Combine all ingredients thoroughly, and store in refrigerator in a covered jar. Before using, shake well. Can be used as a marinade or as a basting sauce for steak.

KING OF THE ROAD BARBECUE SAUCE (Table Sauce)

2 8-oz. cans tomato
   sauce
⅔ cup chopped Spanish
   onion
⅓ tsp. salt
½ tsp. freshly ground
   pepper

3 tsp. sugar
2 tbs. wine vinegar
1 tbs. tarragon vinegar
1 ½ tsp. Worcestershire
   sauce
2 dashes Tobasco sauce
½ tsp. lemon juice

Combine all ingredients in a covered skillet and simmer slowly about 30 minutes or until onion is tender. Store in a covered jar in the refrigerator. This sauce is especially good on hamburger or flank steaks. Makes about 2 cups.

BEARNAISE SAUCE

3 shallots
1 sprig fresh parsley
½ tsp. tarragon
½ tsp. chervil
4 tbs. wine vinegar

2 tbs. water
4 egg yolks
4 tbs. butter
Salt to taste
Dash of cayenne pepper

In saucepan, mix vinegar with water and cook shallots, parsley, tarragon and chervil. Bring to boil and cook about 3 minutes, strain. Add this herb liquid, a little at a time, to the egg yolks in the upper part of a double boiler, stirring constantly. Cook over hot water, stirring constantly until sauce thickens. Add the butter, blend well, then add salt and few grains of cayenne pepper.

STEAK TOPPER AND GLORIFIER (Table Sauce)

Flour
4 tbs. butter or
   margarine
⅔ lb. mushrooms

⅔ tsp. soy sauce
½ tsp. Worcestershire
Salt
Freshly ground pepper

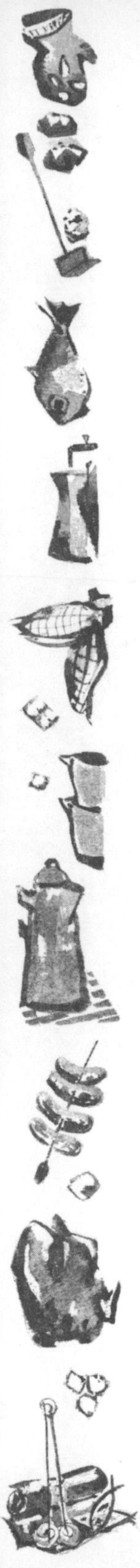

Wash mushrooms, and if desired, slice them. Sprinkle lightly with flour and saute mushrooms in butter about 9 to 12 minutes, or until tender. Add remaining ingredients and cook just until heated. Serve hot over steaks. About 5 servings.

BASIC BARBECUE SANDWICH SAUCE (Table Sauce)

1 whole onion, minced	1 large can tomatoes
1 clove of garlic, minced	with puree, sieved
2 tbs. salad oil	¼ cup cider vinegar
1 ½ tsp. chili powder	2 tbs. sugar
¼ tsp. turmeric	½ tsp. celery salt
½ tsp. dry mustard	¼ tsp. cayanne pepper
2 bay leaves	or Tobasco sauce
¼ tsp. marjoram	

In heavy skillet, saute the garlic and onion in oil for about 6 minutes. Add the remaining ingredients and simmer gently, stirring occasionally, about 30 to 45 minutes until mixture reaches desired consistancy. Remove the bay leaves before serving. May be used hot or cold. This barbecue sauce is not to be used for basting, but served over meats (good for leftovers) and in sandwiches.. Makes a little over 2 cups. Sauce may be sealed in jars.

LAMB BARBECUE SAUCE (Table Sauce)

¾ cup mayonnaise	1 tsp. celery salt
¼ cup wine vinegar	½ tsp. freshly ground
1 6-oz. can tomato paste	pepper
2 tbs. Worcestershire	½ tsp. cayenne pepper
1 tbs. A-1 Steak sauce	½ tsp. Tabasco sauce
2 tbs. chopped onion	1 tbs. fresh parsley,
1 ¼ tbs. horse radish	ground

Blend all ingredients well and store in covered jar in refrigerator. Makes about 2 cups. Good on all red meats as well as lamb.

SWEET & SOUR SAUCE
(Table sauce)

3 tbs. corn starch	⅓ cup water
1¼ cups pineapple juice	½ cup brown sugar
1 tbs. soy sauce	2 cups pineapple chunks
3 tbs. wine vinegar	2 green peppers, chopped

Blend all ingredients except pineapple chunks and green pepper, and cook until thickened, stirring constantly. Add pineapple and pepper and cook 5 minutes longer, or until fruit thoroughly heated. Serve with pork, lamb, poultry and kebobs.

BURGER RELISH

½ cup catsup
1 small can tomato paste
⅓ cup pickle relish
¼ cup cider vinegar
⅓ cup sugar

1 tbs. unsulphured
molasses
1 medium onion,
chopped (optional)
2 tsp. prepared mustard
½ tsp. salt

Combine all ingredients in saucepan, bring to boil. Reduce heat and simmer about 5 minutes, stirring occasionally. Serve hot or cold with burgers or franks. Makes about 2 ¼ cups.

MEXICAN "SALSA" RELISH

5 or 6 medium tomatoes
3 large onions
1 4-oz. can green chilis,
seeded
2 tbs. red wine vinegar

¼ cup olive oil
¼ tsp. cumin (comino)
¼ oregano
salt to taste

Mince the tomatoes, onions, and green chilis. Add remaining ingredients and mix well. Place in refrigerator at least 2 hours to let flavors blend before using. Serve as relish for any red meat.

POLISH RELISH

2 cups cooked beets,
minced
⅓ cup prepared horse-
radish
1 tbs. sugar

1 tbs. wine vinegar
1 tsp. salt
Dash of pepper
Pinch of cayenne pepper

Combine all ingredients in covered container. Store in refrigerator 2 or 3 days before using. Mix well before serving with pork, corned beef or roast beef. Makes about 2 ½ cups relish.

CABBAGE RELISH

1 small head cabbage,
finely shredded
⅓-¼ cup celery, minced
1 large green pepper,
minced

½ cup sugar
½ cup cider vinegar
1 tsp. salt, or to taste
½ tsp. onion salt
¼ tsp. pepper

Mix all ingredients well. Chill before serving in covered container. This relish will keep several days in the refrigerator. Excellent with seafood and most meats. Makes about 1 quart.

Index To Recipes

Meat Recipes which may be prepared with more than one kind of meat (see page 24) are cross-indexed.

QUICK KEY TO BARBECUE MEAT VARIETY

Each recipe title in the Meat Chapter is accompanied by one or more of the above symbols. They denote the variety of meats which may be used with the recipe, for easy and immediate identification. The symbols, for beef, lamb and pork, appear in a sequence which shows the most popularly used meat closest to the recipe title. The following symbols are recommended alternatives. Check recipes for possible changes in cooking times, handling and seasonings between meat varieties.

Other PACIFICA HOUSE Books:

The Pacifica House HAWAII COOK BOOK — Title 101

The Pacifica House CHEESE BOOK — Title 102

Young Folk's Hawaiian Time (children's stories) — Title 201

Send For Your
BARBECUE COLLEGE DIPLOMA

Chef Bell would like to award a handsome graduation diploma to each reader who has studied his Barbecue College Course in the front of the book. Beautifully lithographed on parchment, and suitable for framing, the diploma bestows upon the recipient, the honorary degree of Master of Barbecuing. Each is hand-lettered with the graduate's name and signed by Chef Bell. Simply read the 25 statements below and check them "True" or "False" on the tear-off tab. No minimum score is required, though each examination will be graded. Be sure to fill in the name and address box. Tear off the tab and mail to Ed Bell's Barbecue College. A nominal charge of 50¢ is requested for each examination to cover costs of processing and postage. Please allow 3 to 4 weeks for return delivery.

TEAR HERE

Please send me my Barbecue College Diploma. I enclose the answers to the examination, along with 50¢ for processing and postage.

Name (Please print clearly or type)

Address

City   State   Zip Code

Mail to:

ED BELL'S BARBECUE COLLEGE
10000 Riverside Drive
North Hollywood, Calif.

	TRUE	FALSE	
1. Barbecue cooking is modern America's major contribution to the world of culinary arts.			1.
2. An important contribution to barbecue cooking was made by the early settlers of Western America.			2.
3. The most important factor in good-flavored barbecuing is the fuel.			3.
4. Of the four basic types of barbecue units, the deluxe covered unit, or barrel is most versatile.			4.
5. Sturdy construction is important in barbecue equipment selection, for reliability and safety.			5.
6. The maximum weight of roasts and turkeys for motorized spit cooking is 12 pounds.			6.
7. Cooking with charcoal is not recommended for unventilated indoor use.			7.

	TRUE	FALSE	
8.			8. All charcoal briquets are the same — as long as they are made of wood.
9.			9. Charcoal briquets will be ready for cooking 20 to 30 minutes after starting with an electric starter unit.
10.			10. Improper use of starter fuels and inferior briquets can result in unpleasant food flavoring.
11.			11. Proper preparation of fire bowl or pan with foil and gravel helps eliminate cooking flareups, prolongs equipment life.
12.			12. All weights and sizes of aluminum foil are recommended for barbecue use.
13.			13. Covered barbecue units require more charcoal than open units.
14.			14. The ash which forms on burning briquets does not effect the cooking temperature.
15.			15. When spit cooking on an open braizer with hood and motor, the temperature is controlled by raising and lowering the spit level.
16.			16. The average temperature for spit and covered barbecue cooking is 325°F.
17.			17. Grill cooking heat is controlled by the amount of fuel used — how close together it is, and the distance between fuel and food.
18.			18. Barbecue seasoning should complement foods— not cover up natural flavors.
19.			19. Marinades are primarily for seasoning meats and have little effect on tenderness.
20.			20. A foil drip pan is used to catch juices and cooking sauces when grilling steaks.
21.			21. A grill should always be oiled with the same oil as is used in the cooking sauce or rubbed onto the food.
22.			22. The best cuts of meat for barbecuing come from the loin section.
23.			23. Use of a meat thermometer is the most accurate way to tell when barbecued roasts are done.
24.			24. Hickory chips to be tossed in the coals for flavoring should be soaked at least 30 minutes in cold water before using.
25.			25. The best time to clean your barbecue unit is the day after it was used.

TEAR HERE

Examination score